AROUND TADLEY
people and places

Tadley and District History Society

A charabanc outing to Bournemouth in
the early 1920s. The local fixed price
for this trip in 1923 was 8/6d (43p)
a not inconsiderable sum in those days.
This charabanc is a converted ex-War
Department Thorneycroft lorry capable of
12 mph – a journey time in excess of
5 hours each way!

Names: 1: May Saunders, 2: William
'Chummy' Bowman, 3: ? Bowman,
4: George 'Curly' Saunders, 5: Ernie
Bowman with sons Stan and Reg,
6: Mrs Alice Bowman (wife of Ernie).

Published by Tadley and District History Society (TADS)
PO Box 7264, Tadley RG26 3FA, United Kingdom.

First published November 2001.

Layout, design and pre-press TADS.

Digital preparation TADS and Steve Gardner.

Software Adobe Photoshop and Adobe InDesign.

Typefaces The main text is set in 9 on 10 point Adobe Minion;
chapter headings are set in 34 on 36 point Adobe Christiana.

Cover design The project committee, with special thanks to Jo Stevens.

Printing and binding produced through AB Print, Wokingham,
Berkshire.

Further copies of this and other TADS publications may be obtained
by writing to Tadley and District History Society, PO Box 7264,
Tadley RG26 3FA, United Kingdom.

ISBN 0 9537043 2 7

Tadley and District History Society gratefully
acknowledge financial support from Hampshire
County Council and the National Lottery's Awards
for All scheme.

Supported by
Hampshire
County
Council

AWARDS
FOR ALL

Photographic acknowledgements

© British Crown Copyright 2001/MOD material is reproduced
with the permission of the controller of Her Britannic Majesty's
Stationery Office.

© English Heritage material is reproduced by permission of
English Heritage.

Francis Frith Collection material is reproduced with permission
of the Francis Frith Collection, Salisbury, Wiltshire SP3 5QP,
www.francisfrith.co.uk

Vickers Collection material is reproduced with permission of
Rolls-Royce plc, Derby.

Contents

Introduction

Tadley and District History Society (TADS) was founded in 1984 for people with an interest in local social history, and in the broader scope of history and natural history. Monthly evening talks are arranged, usually on the third Wednesday of each month, except August, at St Paul's Church Hall, Tadley. There is also an annual coach outing and occasional local walks.

Current membership numbers seventy and meetings are open to visitors.

The society has published a number of local history booklets, and reproduced several older out-of-print publications of significance to the area. A list of all current TADS publications, together with ordering details may be obtained by writing to: Tadley and District History Society, PO Box 7264, Tadley RG26 3FA, United Kingdom.

TADS is a member of Hampshire Archives Trust which is associated with Hampshire Public Record Office.

For further information and programme details contact:
Bob Brown tel: 0118 981 6109 or
Derek Ward tel: 0118 981 2626;
email: dgward@bigfoot.com

Following the success of the Tadley & District History Society (TADS) millennium publication *Around Tadley – fact and fable*, we were offered many family and local photographs. These, together with the ones not used for the book, prompted the society to begin research on this new publication, *Around Tadley – people and places*.

Modern conventional photography using negatives was introduced in 1839 by William Fox Talbot. In the early days the equipment used was heavy and cumbersome and exposure times were lengthy, making it necessary for people in the photographs to be still for a long time – hence the unsmiling portraits of many Victorian families. By the 1840s commercial photographers were well established in towns, specialising in studio portraits, *cartes de visite* and topographical views. In 1894 the Post Office permitted the sending of these views through the post and the public took to sending 'picture postcards', rather as we use the telephone or e-mail to-day – a quick and cheap way to communicate with friends and relatives. The advent of roll film and box cameras greatly increased the availability and popularity of photography and today many local families have their own collections of old photographs to which the society has been privileged to have access. Because of the popularity of photography during the last one hundred years, we are fortunate to be able to create a fascinating record of social history, using a mix of commercial, professional and personal photographs.

Situated in north Hampshire, Tadley has grown dramatically in recent years – from a small rural village into quite a substantial town. This book is a photographic record not a history; it seeks to illustrate what life was like in the past, highlighting some of the changes that have occurred in the past hundred years during its growth.

Around Tadley – people and places has been arranged under subject headings. We have identified events, places, and the names of people where possible, but we have not been able to provide complete records. Every effort has been made to ensure that names are spelt correctly; we apologise for any inaccuracies that may have occurred where we had to depend on personal memories. If any readers can provide information to fill in some of the gaps we would like to be informed.

We hope that this publication will stimulate further offers of photographs of local interest, including ones taken in more recent years which will soon be of interest to the present generation, and future local historians.

The Project Team, October 2001

AROUND TADLEY
people and places

Childhood and education

© Gazette Newspapers, Basingstoke

↑ Outside Buckingham Palace on 23 November 1995 – Joyce Lambden proudly displays her MBE, awarded to her in the Queen's Birthday Honours List.

Childhood and education are clearly linked; in a sense children going to school has made the distinction between child and adult much more apparent. Before the introduction of compulsory education children were expected to play an important role in the running of the family – looking after younger brothers and sisters, or working alongside adults. Indeed the school summer holiday is a legacy of the days when children were needed to help in the busiest season of the agricultural year. In October 1922 the Tadley School Headmaster complained that 1242 attendances had been lost due to hop picking. There were however times when children were free to play. Clothes might be hand-me-downs, toys scarce, and television unimagined, but like rural children everywhere Tadley children had trees to climb, a brook to fish in, and quiet roads and common land to wander. Life for children was often not idyllic, they were vulnerable to diseases that are today preventable or curable; life for some could be brutally short.

Up until 1870 it was left to individuals, usually women, or voluntary societies usually religious, to provide a basic education for those who wanted or could afford it. Tadley is recorded as having both a Dame School and a British School. Following the 1870 Education Act, Primary Schools were established in most areas and Tadley Board School opened its doors to its first intake of 151 children in April 1877. For many of these children this brought into their lives a new authority figure – the teacher. Some of the older people who went to school in the years following World War I, clearly remember one of them, Mr Miller, for his strictness and ideas of discipline.

With the development of Tadley after the World War II came the need for more schools. In the early 1950s this resulted in what is now 'The Den' being used as an annexe to Tadley School. Pupils later transferred to wartime huts in Newchurch Road and eventually to the purpose-built Burnham Copse Schools. To cater for Tadley's ever expanding population the Bishopwood Schools opened in 1972. The 1944 Education Act instructed local authorities to provide secondary education in a separate school for pupils up to the age of 15, according to 'age, aptitude and ability'. Consequently in 1957 The Hurst County Secondary School opened with 381 pupils, while those who passed the 11+ examination went either to the Grammar School in Basingstoke or Newbury. In 1971 The Hurst became a Comprehensive and later a Community School.

Nowadays instead of playing in the countryside and lanes, children play on the slides and frames of modern playgrounds, take part in the many organised clubs, and often find their entertainment through sophisticated electronic toys. School is compulsory until 16 and in common with youngsters everywhere many Tadley children go on to university – something few of their great-grandparents would have thought possible.

Tadley Board School opened in 1876 and for 75 years was the only school in the village. Now known as Tadley Community Primary School, many of the original buildings are still in use.

↑ An early 20th century photograph of the front of the school taken from The Green. Notice the bell tower, which was later dismantled when it became unsafe.

← A photograph taken in 1909, this time from the rear of the school. It shows the divided playground, segregating the boys from the girls.

← An early 1950s photograph also from the playground. No longer segregated, it is now tarmaced. The temporary HORAS classrooms erected in 1947 can be seen on the left hand side. Notice also the bell tower has been removed.

↑ A photograph from about 1916 of children at Tadley School with the Master's wife, Mrs Follett, on the right hand side. Others in the photograph include, back row (l to r): Ethel Smith, Violet Simpson, Fred Bowman, Tom Stacey, H West, Alf Bruce, Florrie Stacey, Audrey Randall; middle row: L West, S West, Violet Appleton, ?, Cissie Appleton, Dorrie Chapple, A Smith, D West; bottom row: Eva West, V Rogers, Mollie Saunders, Lilly Simpson, Rose West, Nancy Chapple, Katie Chapple, C Appleton.

← A photograph from about 1915 of Master, Mr Joseph Follett, and his wife.

↑ (top) This photograph, taken in 1921-22, shows Walter Miller (left) shortly after he was appointed Master of Tadley School, replacing Henry Follett. Back row (l to r): Jim Smith, Jim Saunders, Walter Chapman, Maud Chapman, Gwen ?, Lucy Green, Frank Hawkins, Stan West; middle back row: Len Boyd, Jack Goddard, Olive Absolom, Rose Chapman, Gladys Durrant, Annie Chapman, 'Sis' Stacey, Len Butler, Ted Nash; middle front row: Jack Smith, Eddie Turrell, George Wigley, Nancy Middleton, Stella Monger, Doris Kimber, 'Sis' West, Rose West; front row: Rebecca Nash, Mary Long, Mabel West, 'Sis' Smith, Nellie Benham.

↑ (bottom) A rare view of the inside of a Tadley School classroom in the 1930s. Walter Miller (far left) is still Master with assistant, Miss Crief (centre). For names see page 142.

↑ Mr Murphy's class of 1951.
Back row (l to r): Vesta Bowles,
June West, Pam Saunders, Jean
Woodcock, Eileen Cripps,
Shirley West, Joyce Forsberg;
middle standing: Brian Long,
Ted Englefield, George Stacey,
Brian Loader, David James,
Bob Ebsworth, Ken Saunders,
Billy Helyar, Brian Lambden,
Roy West; middle seated: John
Edwards, Bill Saunders,
Desmond Smith, Lilian Pike
Barbara Bailey, Cynthia
Gillingham, Dorothy Pike,
John 'Jackie' Caple, Mike
'Tinker' Taylor, Mike Moss;
front row: John Broom, Brian
Phillis, Peter Sutherland,
George Hiscock.

← Dancing practice in the
playground during the summer
of 1952-53 (note the absence of
boys!). Country dancing is still
a summer activity at the school
today with pupils putting on
displays for parents at fêtes
and entering competitions with
other local schools.

In 1976, Tadley School, by now known as Tadley County Primary School, celebrated its centenary. Children dressed up in traditional Victorian clothes and past pupils were invited back to join in the celebrations.

↑ Class teacher, Mrs Eileen Wood, with her pupils – smiling happy faces, unlike most Victorian photographs! Back row (l to r): James Napleton, ?, Kirsty Jennings, Carl Bridger, Mandy ?, Elizabeth ?; middle row: Rachel James, ?, Patrick Maleperiman, Scott ?, Thomas Gowers; front row: Clive Stacey, Christopher Mitchell, Darren Saunders, Roger Hailey.

← Four past pupils enjoying the centenary celebrations (l to r): Mrs Ellen Clark, Mrs Blanche Bowman, Mrs May Lay and Mrs Wigley.

With the arrival of the Atomic Weapons Research Establishment (AWRE) in the early 1950s came the need for a school in north Tadley. For several years an annexe to Tadley School operated in 'The Den' – the old World War II airfield gunnery and crew procedure building.

↑ (top) An early 1950s photograph of 'The Den' when part of the building was being used as an annexe to Tadley School. Notice the air-raid shelter on the left hand side of the photograph.

↑ (bottom) A 1952 class photograph taken in 'The Den'.

© *Rural History Centre, The University of Reading*

On 5 September 1955 the juniors were transferred from the overcrowded Tadley School annexe to the 'Chivers Hostel' dining area (another World War II airfield building) in Newchurch Road, to await the building of the new Burnham Copse Junior School.

↑ (top) A 1950s photograph of the 'Chivers Hostel', now Searing Way. The new road was named after the school's first Headteacher, Roger Searing.

↑ (bottom) Following the opening of the Burnham Copse Junior School in 1960 the infants transferred from 'The Den' annexe to the vacated 'Chivers Hostel' site. A 1966/67 Burnham Copse Infant School photograph taken at the hostel. For names see page 142.

In June 1960 the newly built Burnham Copse Junior School buildings were occupied.

↑ Roger Searing, headmaster, presenting Kathy Smallwood with a trophy for girl athlete of the year in 1971. Her outstanding athletic talent continued throughout her school years and at Loughborough University. She became a member of the UK athletics team and married Gary Cook, a fellow team member.

← The 1976 gymnastics team. Back row (l to r): Paul March, Richard Halliwell, Denise Younge, Wendy Shoulder, Jo Copeland, Eira Jones, Poppy Anthony, Joanne ?; front row: Nina Ingle, Leanne Waterman, Susannah Bond, Emma Harvey, ?, Angela Stacey, Elizabeth Wingrove, Justine Carter, Tina Gardham, Paula Newman.

↑ This picture shows Burnham Copse Infant School, Newchurch Road, under construction in 1984. Nicknamed the 'Wigwam School', because of its unusual shape, it received a design award; the architect was Ian Templeton.

← Kathy Cook planting a commemorative tree at the school's tenth birthday celebrations. An ex-pupil of the old school, Kathy won athletic medals at Olympic, European and Commonwealth events, and has held the British record for 400m for the last 17 years. She was awarded the MBE at the end of her athletics career.

Bishopswood Infant School opened in April 1972. It was built on old withy beds and is close to the Bishopswood stream which led to serious disruption from flooding in its early years.

↑ In 1996-98 the infants participated in a display of pupils' work at the Sun Life of Canada building in Basingstoke town centre. Head teacher Christine Neald and Jenny Higginson are seen here with pupils.

← Year 2 pupils (1995-96), keen to get the feel of life in Victorian times, dress up in costume for a school project entitled *Finding out about History*. Deputy head, Marilyn Penman is seen here with her class.

© *Gazette Newspapers, Basingstoke*

Bishopswood Junior School was opened in January 1972, three months before the Infant School.

↑ (top) Modern education strives to provide opportunities for pupils to benefit through self-expression and enjoyment. A good example is this 1989 production of *Charlie and the Chocolate Factory*; (l to r) Zoe Jones, Meena Ram, Nicola Flaxman, Amy Norman, Nathan Quelch, Colin Simmons.

↑ (bottom) Junior school staff at the time of the above production. Back row (l to r): Diana Golding, Ruth Carman, Carol Milne, Pam Baker, Joan Thomas; front row: Pam Miller, Mary Parrott, Wendy Rawlings (Headteacher), Hazel Chalk, Josie Jones.

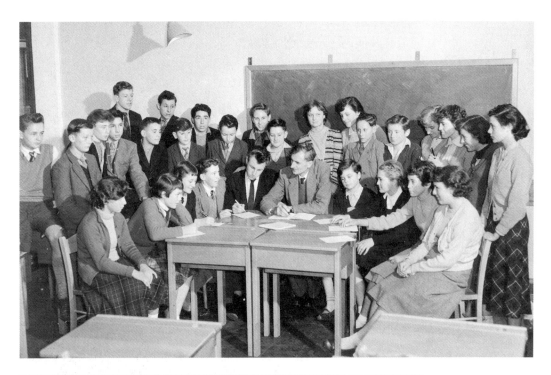

In September 1957, amid building rubble and debris, 381 pupils joined the newly opened Hurst County Secondary School. It became a comprehensive school in the early 1970s and a community school in 1979.

↑ (top) The democratic process operated at the Hurst School from the outset. Here the School Council, comprising representatives from each form, discuss matters of concern with Headmaster, Maurice Bound.

↑ (bottom) The official opening ceremony on 16 September 1958 performed by His Grace The Duke of Wellington, Lord Lieutenant of Hampshire.

To celebrate the 40th Anniversary of the opening of the Hurst School a photographic record of school life was made during the Autumn Term 1997.

↑ Seen here are (l to r) Gregory Speed, Philip Spray, Kathy Lamb, and Richard Alvis conducting an experiment in the science laboratory.

← On Sunday 14 December the school held its 40th Anniversary Concert. Organised and co-ordinated by the Hurst PTA together with James Paterson, parent, who was at that time, resident director of *Phantom of the Opera* at Her Majesty's Theatre, London. Pictured here is James (second from right) with musical colleagues from Phantom who joined him in the concert.

© Gazette Newspapers, Basingstoke

Guide companies and Brownie packs were established in the area by the 1930s. However a confirmed date for the formation of Tadley groups does not appear until after World War II.

↑ A letter to the Queen telling her that her 40th wedding anniversary coincided with 1st Tadley Brownies' 40th birthday, paved the way for a trip of a lifetime to Buckingham Palace for the entire pack in November 1987. This happy photograph, taken on the coach, shows the pack with Guiders Heather Alliston, Clare Best, 'Jenny' Jennings and Freda Keel (front), Gwen Goode (centre), and Nancy Jones and Sarah Goodchild (back right).

← A photograph of 1st Tadley Guides in the mid-1950s, taken by Sarah Branson. The occasion was Commonwealth Day and the company had marched to Pamber Priory for the commemorative service. Sarah was later to become Commissioner for all England and the Guide Advisor for Commonwealth Headquarters.

↑ (top) Six years after the Scout movement was founded by Baden Powell in 1908, Tadley had its own troop of 12 boys. Whether the troop continued to meet during World War I is not known. Older Tadley people do remember a troop, with a band, being run by Miss Marshall, proprietor of Barn Close Laundry, in the post war period (see page 69). This photograph is believed to show that troop in 1922.

↑ (bottom) The present group began as the 26th Basingstoke in 1955 and met at the Old Community Centre in Newchurch Road. This camp photograph of the 26th Wolf Cub pack was taken at Coombe in 1961. Leaders, back row (l to r): ? , Avril Kent, Akela Michael Mullender, ? , Barbara Feuillade, Jim Cook.

Streets and lanes

These days, it is easy to drive from Tadley to Bath, London, the South Coast, and many other places; people 'nip in' to Basingstoke, Newbury, or Reading to do their shopping. However this mobility has been bought at a price as the population of Tadley has grown. The tranquil scenes of streets and lanes on the following pages clearly show that the price has been the loss of safety, silence, and freedom. Children can no longer wander up Tadley Hill on the A340. Mothers would not today push their prams up Dix Hill and it would be most unusual to see a solitary car drive through Tadley! Not that these roads were always as safe as they appear. On the 19 March 1928 Tadley School was closed so that children could attend the funeral of a fellow pupil, who was accidentally killed by a car, ten minutes after leaving school.

The ways in which lanes and streets have been altered to accommodate motor vehicles and an increased population often makes it difficult to identify them in old photographs. Who for example, without the caption, could readily identify Trunkpond Corner, Bowman's Brook, or even Mulfords Hill? It often comes as a surprise to find how relatively recent some of these changes have been. As late as the 1970s children trudged or walked (depending on their attitude) up Fairlawn Road to school without the security of a pavement. Only thirty years ago Gutteridge Lane was still an overgrown track that ran alongside a pig farm. After 1956 traffic through Tadley was controlled by a 30 mph speed limit but it went unregulated, without traffic lights or roundabout, until the 1980s.

The following photographs show how simple the early streets and lanes of Tadley were compared to today. There is little clutter of street furniture: streetlights, road signs, or instructions to control motorists. Instead of kerbs, drains and tarmac there are grass verges, ditches and gravel. The noise of wheels on these gravelled lanes gave greater warning of approaching vehicles, and to broom-makers awaiting orders this could be 'music to their ears'.

Despite all the changes, the streets and lanes of Tadley still retain echoes of the past – if only in their names, which often reveal previous residents, local worthies, or some long gone geographical feature. Within a short distance of the busy A340 it is still possible, however briefly, to imagine yourself in a tranquil, rural Tadley before the motor car. To walk along Church Road, Rimes Lane, Malthouse Lane, or West Street is to remind yourself of what most of the village was like in the early part of the 20th century. One can also reflect on what we have lost of that peaceful, unhurried world, when it was safe enough to wander home in the middle of the road.

↑ Tombstone of the local benefactor, John Mulford whose memory is perpetuated in the local road bearing his name. He died on 7 January 1814, aged 94 and is buried in the graveyard of Mortimer West End Chapel. The epitaph on the stone reads, *Gone to know more, adore more, love more; Christ victorious. Satan vanquished. Here on earth take thy part of John Mulford.*

Dix Hill. Tadley. 2052.

Post Office Rd, Tadley. 2056.

↑ Approaching a virtually traffic free Tadley from Basingstoke. A pre-1930 photograph with the road (now the A340) still unsurfaced. The building on the left is The Fighting Cocks public house (see page 35).

← Another pre-1930 view, continuing up the hill, now known as Main Road. The Primitive Methodist Chapel is the low roofed building in the centre, now a private house (see page 62). The cottage by the bend in the road was demolished for a road improvement scheme which was never implemented.

← A view familiar to older residents. On the left is Stacey's shop (page 74), later a Post Office and now a private house; on the right is Allen's Garage (see page 73), an ex-army building since demolished. Just beyond on the other side of the road is Thick's Bakery, later Smith and Eyres and finally Pikes (both general stores) before being demolished for private housing.

© Rural History Centre, The University of Reading

↑ Looking north down Tadley Hill in the early 1920s, with a group of youngsters obviously posing for the photographer. On the right of the picture is a heap of gravel used for filling potholes in the unsurfaced road.

← Taken from approximately the same position around the same time as the top picture, but looking south up Tadley Hill. In the distance is Stacey's shop (see page 74). Opposite, on the extreme left and just visible, is the old Forge, later the Post Office sorting office, now demolished. Note the absence of Allens Garage on the left.

← This picture is also looking south up Tadley Hill, with Pound Cottage on the immediate left. This is a more recent photograph of the A340, showing the road now surfaced, but before the bends were straightened and the roundabout built.

↑ An early 20th century view looking south from the bottom of Mulfords Hill. The building in the distance was known as Elmhurst. In the 1930s Commander Christie lived there and by the 1950s Mr & Mrs Fox who ran a riding school. Tadley's swimming pool was built on part of the site. The road to the right was re-routed to the south as New Road.

← A 1930s view taken from Trunk Pond Corner (Rowan Road), now the roundabout, looking towards Mulfords Hill. On the right are the the the old railway carriages; in the foreground is the Pound and the War memorial (page 124).

← A view looking west along New Road. The house on the left was demolished in 2001. It was once occupied by local photographer James Thatcher and later by Police Constable Mead.

MULFORD'S HILL TADLEY

Mulfords Hill, Tadley. 2   T.H.B.

↑ A photograph from about 1909, looking north up Mulfords Hill. The large building on the right is the Salvation Army Hall (see page 66). The thatched cottage in front of it has since been demolished and is now the site of Bridge Court.

← A pre-1930s view looking south down Mulfords Hill – the road is now surfaced. The Salvation Army Hall is on the left with a row of some of Tadley's earliest council houses on the right.

← An earlier picture, taken from the brow of Mulfords Hill looking south. The first building on the left, just past the group of walkers, is George West's broomyard (see page 85). Behind the railings on the left, the Williams family used to set up their fairground ride at the beginning of the season and let the local children have rides (see page 42). This area is now known as Gorselands.

↑ (top) Looking south down Mulfords Hill towards Basingstoke – The Fox and Hounds public house (see page 36) and Mount Pleasant are on the right. Opposite them is Blake's shop (see page 76), later Lowes and then Whatmores. Pilgrims Cottage lies just beyond it. All these properties have been demolished in recent years. The Budgens Supermarket complex is now sited there.

↑ (bottom) A view from the top of Mulfords Hill looking south. The large house on the left is now Poulters Estate Agents. Blakes Lane is just beyond the site of the next cottage.

Bowman's Brook, Tadley.

↑ (top) This pre-1928 view of
Bowman's Brook looking north shows
the ford and the wooden footbridge.
Pamber Heath Road is beyond the ford
on the right and West Street is off to
the left. The post box in the centre of
the picture was resited in the 1960s
when the Rowan Road estate was built.

↑ (bottom) A similar view to the top
photograph, but taken in the 1950s
after the ford had been bridged. Iron
railings replaced the former wooden
ones over the ford sometime after 1928
and those on the right are still there.
Rowan Road is on the left, Fairlawn
Road is in the foreground and the
pathway to the right is Sandy Lane.

© *Rural History Centre, The University of Reading*

↑ A view looking eastward along East Street (now Franklin Avenue) towards the Mulfords Hill-Silchester Road junction. The first house on the left was occupied by the Englefield family and later extended to include the barber's shop. It is now known as Emit House (see page 75).

← A view looking west along East Street (Franklin Avenue). Pine View, the house on the left, next to the present day Co-op, was owned by Robert Goddard and family in the 1920s. More recently, the premises have been used as an estate agents, gunshop, a café run by Sonner Black, a carpet shop and finally a charity shop.

← A view from Newtown Common looking north towards Pine View. The trees, known as 'Peaky' Firs, were part of Aldermaston Estate and were removed during World War II to make way for Aldermaston Airfield (page 127).

HEATH END
BAUGHURST

Heath End, Baughurst

Heath End has always been a part of the parish of Tadley. Previously 'cut off' from the early village by a swathe of heathland, the building of the AWRE housing estates has helped to integrate the hamlet into the parish.

↑ Appleton's cart shed with broom sheds behind, which were situated at the junction of Heath End Road and Bishopswood Lane

← To commemorate the Coronation of George VI in 1937 Jean Butler (née Kent), as the youngest pupil at Baughurst School, was chosen to plant a poplar tree on the corner of Heath End Road and Brimpton Road. She was assisted by Mrs Kendrick. The previous poplar, a landmark for many years, was reduced to a 1.5 metre stump as the result of a storm.

← By the 1950s the tree was once again a local landmark but it also came to an untimely end when, in the 1960s, it was removed as part of road widening to enable buses to turn more easily.

↑ Believed to be a view from what is now the Calleva Industrial Park roundabout with present day AWE on the left, Calleva Park on the right and Heath End Road directly in front.

→ This is a view looking north along Heath End Road with The Cricketers ale house sign on the right (see page 34). The photograph was probably taken about 1920 and shows just how dense the wooded, mainly pine, areas were.

→ A later photograph taken in the 1950s. The road is now better surfaced and there is an absence of pine trees in the distance as a result of clearance for the building of the airfield during World War II.

Leisure and sport

Whether you approach Tadley from Reading, Basingstoke or Newbury one of the first buildings you see is one that makes English life and leisure distinctive. That building is of course the public house or 'pub', each with its own atmosphere and regular customers. As the photographs show, the facades of these pubs have altered little over the years, but inside they have adapted to changing lifestyles. All have lost their public bars; it is no longer possible for children to buy crisps or pop in a 'snug' bar at The Fighting Cocks or The New Inn. Indeed, when Bill Saunders was landlord of The New Inn you could also order coal in the bar from his coalyard at the back. Tadley has also lost some of its pubs – The Rampant Cat in Fairlawn Road, The Malthouse in Malthouse Lane and The Star on Dix Hill – but what the pubs provide remains as popular as ever, including the traditional game of darts (see page 32).

In the past, rural communities often had to make their own entertainment and organise their own celebrations. The photographs of festivities on pages 40-41 are typical scenes that illustrate the charming simplicity of these occasions enjoyed by Tadley people – both young and old – in the summers of long ago. However, in recent times enterprising individuals have continued to organise activities in the town; the Lighthouse Bus and Tadley Watch, featured in this chapter, are just two examples of this.

Nowadays cars provide the means for regular days out, but in the 1920s and 1930s a coach or charabanc trip to Southsea was often the only trip of the year. The many photographs of these trips loaned, but which for reasons of space we could not include in this book, indicate how popular they were. The absence of men in the photographs shows that opportunities for leisure activities were often restricted to those who could take time off from work.

Organised sport, particularly football and cricket, has been a feature of Tadley life for over a century, with The Green at times the arena for both. To play football on The Green in the depths of winter with two inches of glutinous mud stuck to your boots and a hardy clutch of supporters offering advice (not always welcome) from the railings may not be everyone's idea of a pleasant experience. Perhaps what often makes local team sport enjoyable and worthwhile, whether it be football, netball, cricket, darts, or anything else, is that it is one of the ways in which people in the local community can come together with a common objective and purpose. Certainly there must be something that has kept people coming to The Green over the years, in all weathers and conditions.

↑ Enjoying a day out – (l to r) Ambrose Allen, George H Stacey and ? Saunders. A coach outing from The Old House at Home public house at Pamber Green, prior to its de-licensing in 1956.

↑ Tadley football team, 1906. Back row (l to r): W Stacey, ? , Alfie Dale, Bunny Saunders (goalie), Fred Smith, Harry Barlow, Mr Wootton, Crawford Beer; front row: Len Stacey, Mr Smith, George H Stacey, Len Ford and Ambrose Allen.

→ The team 30 years later. Back row (l to r): Roy Dent, Dennis Stacey, Billy 'Dabby' Carter, Wesley Saunders, Reg Bowman (goalie), Jack Smith, Arthur Wigley, Ernie Wigley, Mr Stocker (referee), George Lewis; front row: George Long, Fred Hollingshead, Fred Long, Ernie Wootton and Peter Hollingshead.

→ The victorious 1950s team, with their trophies after winning the league and cup double. Back row (l to r): R Boyd, Jack Hinsley, Norman Humphries, John Stroud, Archie Pike (goalie), Brian Dormer, Colin Belcher, Dudley Cook, Fred Hollingshead, George Lewis; front row: Roy West, Jack Aldridge, Max Aldridge, Colin Jeffries and Mervyn Carter.

↑ Tadley International team played in Bishopswood Lane. Here is the side who had just beaten Kelvins 4-3 in the 1957 Basingstoke 'B' cup final; (l to r) Mike Loader, Brian Dormer, Frank Harris (capt), Alan Chivers, Jock Cameron, Jim Anscombe (goalie), Simon Edwards, R Allen, John Hutchins, John Willington and Roy West.

→ This 1950s team were known as the Tadley Veterans, for obvious reasons! Back row: Jack Appleton, Doug Ward, Roy Bowman (goalie), Ken Janoway, John Willington and Les Appleton; front row: Jack Pike, Frank Harris, Ron Ward, Bill Smith and Arthur Savage.

→ Football club dances/social evenings at the Memorial Hall were well supported events in the late 1940s and early 1950s. The ladies are June Davis, Barbara West and Barbara Wallace, whilst among the 'likely lads' are Michael Taylor. Alf Rolfe, Dudley Cook, Max Aldridge, Colin Belcher, John Lindsey, Bob Rolfe, and Brian (Tiddler) Chapple.

AWRE Recreational Society has provided facilities for a wide variety of sports over the years.

↑ The AWRE ladies netball team of 1960, the year they were formed. Back row (l to r): Ann Lambden, Rosemary Harris, Queenie Stennings, Sheila Dyball and Beryl Morse; front row: Barbara West, Pam Cook and Kate Soper.

→ One of the many AWRE hockey teams of the 1970s. It was a popular sport, with mixed and ladies' teams playing as well as mens'. Back row (l to r): ?, ? Priestly, Mike Broad, Nigel Timmins, David Frost, ?; front row: ? Hickmott, ? Allison, Gavin Stones, Roy Courtney, Jimmy Arnall.

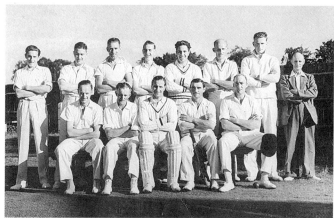

↑ Tadley Cricket Club (date unknown but thought to be the 1910s or 1920s). Back row (l to r): Charlie Lambden, Horace Ward, George Henry Stacey, ?, ? Freeman, ?, Billy Broadhurst and the Revd Ward; front row, Alf West, Dickie Saunders, Ambrose Allen, Bill Upton (wicket keeper) and another unknown player.

← This is the Tadley cricket team in 1957/58. Back row (l to r): Alan Chapple, Dick Harman, Fred Hollingshead, Dudley Cook, Roland Brooks, Geoff Dykes, Vernon Thompson and Arthur Cook (scorer); front row: Tommy Rampton, Bill Rose, Bill Birch, Billy Carter and Ron Ward.

← Another popular local leisure activity is darts. This photograph of the Tadley team is from the early to mid 1950s; (l to r) Joe Cove, Charlie Lane, Vic Hill, Bill Pope, Charlie Bushel and Jim Stamp.

↑ The Falcon public house – a photograph taken about 1932 during the tenancy of the Shatfords who ran the inn from 1928/29 to 1939. Mrs Shatford served bread and cheese at lunch time, a forerunner of the modern 'ploughmans'. The man with his daughter (the taller girl) is the brother of the landlord, visiting in his Austin 7; the smaller girl is the daughter of the house, now Kathleen Gethin.

← A pre-1926 photograph – notice the road is unsurfaced. Interestingly, it is referred to as 'Furzebush Corner' and not the more modern 'Falcon Corner'. The road to Reading bears east. Just to the right of The Falcon was a road leading to Falcon Cottage, thence to Paices Hill, emerging opposite Young's Industrial Estate.

↑ The Cricketers, Heath End has been an inn since at least 1841. Originally an ale/beer house it was not licensed to sell spirits until the 1950s. By 1911 the beer retailer (publican) was Lancelot 'Lance' Richardson. This photograph shows him with his adopted son, Reg, who later (by 1931) became the publican. Notice the two entrances – the bars were totally separate at this time with no inside doorway.

← By the 1960s the right hand bar entrance had been bricked up and further modernisation carried out. The hop logo on the chimney indicates it was a Simonds house at that time.

← Publicans Peggy and John Pippin behind the bar in 1954. They took over the license in 1948/49, when there was still no mains electricity, merely a generator; they made many improvements.

↑ A photograph of The Fighting Cocks public house at the southern end of Tadley, taken about 1924. Although originally thatched it caught fire around 1900 and was rebuilt with a tiled roof. The children are probably on their way home from school.

→ The Vine Hunt setting off from The Fighting Cocks forecourt in the early 1960s. Leading them out is Huntsman Bob James. The Vine and Craven Hunts amalgamated in 1968 but never used this venue. The forecourt was also the starting point of the Remembrance Day parades during this period (see page 125).

© *Rural History Centre, The University of Reading*

↑ View of The Fox and
Hounds public house on
Mulfords Hill, taken from
Whatmore's Garage (now
Wheelgame) in the late 1950s
(see page 78). The large
forecourt of The Fox and
Hounds was used during
World War I as a muster station
where locals assembled prior to
joining the armed forces. It was
also one of the 'stops' on the
Hospital Sunday parade (see
page 111) and headquarters
of the British Legion at its
foundation.

← This view of The New Inn,
Rowan Road, shows George
Wetherall on the left of the
picture. He was the publican
there between 1915–31. The
forecourt of these premises
was used as a meeting point
for local families going hop-
picking (see also pages 90-91).

↑ (top) It was probably a regular sight on a late summer's evening, Sunday or Bank Holiday before the advent of the television to see groups of local 'lads' like this. Hector Benham with his early type motorbike is the only identified member of the group. The motorcycle dates the photograph to pre-1920.

↑ (bottom) A view of Ron Ward's Meadow to the south of Gravelly Close, taken in about 1990. Ron (standing) is talking to a group of adults and children about the wildflowers, animals and insects found in the meadow. Together with Rosemary Bond he founded Tadley 'Watch' Group in 1988.

↑ (top) A rare and early view of the type of utility vehicle in which people were prepared to travel to the coast and back for a glimpse of the seaside. This is an ex-War Department Thorneycroft J-type lorry modified after World War I as a 'lorry-bus'. For names see page 142.

↑ (bottom) The trip to the seaside was a well established event by the time this photograph was taken in 1931/32. It is believed to be a group of 'Old Meeting' worshippers (see page 61). In 1931 new safety regulations were introduced hence the 'EMERGENCY DOOR' sign on this Kent's coach. For names see page 142.

↑ (top) Another outing to Southsea in probably the same 'all-weather' Kent's coach (see page 38). Obviously a dry, warm day enabling passengers to have the top rolled back thus giving us a clear view of the pier in the background. Mrs Ford, organiser of the trip, travelled all the way there and back sat on a cushion in the aisle due to the trip being overbooked! For names see page 143.

↑ (bottom) Believed to be an 1960s outing of Smith and Eyre's employees and their families. Among the group are: driver Alec Milne and his wife Jean, Frank Moss, Nellie Moss, Jean Gundry, Dennis Milne and Hazel Trussler.

TADLEY. MAY DAY 1925

Originally a pagan festival to celebrate the arrival of spring, May Day celebrations with the election of a May Queen became quite a tradition during the Victorian era. Tadley School continued to uphold the traditions in the 1920s with a programme consisting of a procession, crowning, May pole plaiting and numerous dances.

↑ May Day 1925. Amongst the celebrations, Elsie Kimber was elected May Queen and the maids-of-honour, also elected, were: I Hawkins, P Kite, F Englefield, E Mead, L Stacey, P Collier, J Standeven, C West, B Barnes, V Sandford, K Smith, K Cripps, A Cotterill and W Smith. The train bearers were Irene Appleton and Betty Mead, pages of honour William Henstridge (crown bearer), Norman Lambden (garland bearer) and Dennis (wand bearer).

← Rose Queen 1926. Due to the often inclement weather in early May, the event was renamed and held later in the year.

Undoubtedly one of the highlights of the village year was the Tadley Carnival, Fete and Sports day. It was held in the late 1920s on the August Bank Holiday, when most villagers could attend. Competitors assembled at the Recreation Ground before the procession made its way to Hawley Park (see page 101). Horse drawn floats were imaginatively decorated and young and old would dress up in all manner of costumes from the very elaborate to the bizarre. Also known as the Tadley Revel, it was revived after World War II, to raise money for the War Memorial Hall. It was revived again in 1965 and was an annual event for the next 20 years, raising money for local voluntary groups in the area.

↑ → Three photographs of wagons from the events of the 1920s.

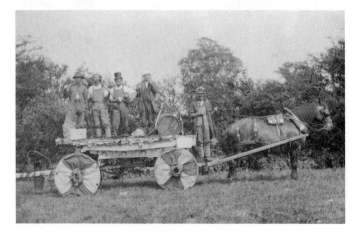

↑ This very early photograph – from about 1905 – was taken at Prospect Park, Reading. It shows several generations of the Williams family, showmen and steam circus proprietors, in front of their gallopers. This was the first season it had been operated by a central steam engine and not 'Grey Tom' the pony. The family used Tadley as their winter quarters for many years and considered it 'home' (see page 22).

← Locals get the opportunity to ride the Williams gallopers. The photograph shows Rose Long (née Anglis) with her young charges. Probably (left) her sister Florrie.

© Reading Evening Post

The Royal Cinema was originally a World War II gunnery-and-crew procedure building. In 1953 part of it was converted into a 270 seat cinema with a 35mm projector. Known as The Royal, in the early sixties Mr Nicholson was the manager. Alan Stiff took over the lease in 1964, running it until 1991 when it finally closed. Bingo and Country dancing continued for a while after the cinema's closure.

← Alan Stiff with Gladys Yarwood, his cashier for many years. Gladys, who doubled as an usherette, died suddenly in February 1993. She was especially remembered by children who attended the Saturday morning shows, for trying to keep them from putting their feet up on the seat in front!

↓ (left) The exterior of *The Royal* during the 1980s.

↓ (right) Regular projectionist Maurice Cooper.

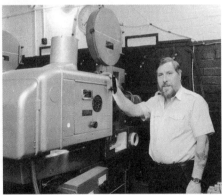

© Reading Evening Post

↑ (top) The Tadley WI was first formed in 1918. Here we see WI President Mrs Annie Thorn carrying out a tree planting ceremony at St Paul's in 1977 to commemorate the Silver Jubilee of Queen Elizabeth II. Others present are Mary Nash, Mrs Paul, Mrs Tudor, Mrs Eyres, Mrs Ethel Everest, Mrs Muriel Baldwin, Mrs Goode and Revd Bill Canham. Tadley WI closed in 1982.

↑ (bottom) Tadley and District Senior Citizens Club at the Memorial Hall. The club began in 1965 with Mrs Marjorie West as the first chairman. A mini-bus, presented by The Bonhomie Club, enabled members to make a range of social visits. The club also catered for the welfare of its members ie chiropody, Meals on Wheels etc.

© Gazette Newspapers, Basingstoke

↑ (top) In May 1973 the ancient ceremony of 'beating the bounds' was revived after 49 years, to raise money towards new instruments for Tadley Band. The ten mile walk began from the forecourt of The Fighting Cocks – for obvious reasons (see page 35)!

↑ (bottom) The distinctive blue and yellow Lighthouse Trust bus, sited in Budgens car park, offered refreshment and friendship to its many customers. It won a bronze medal in the Queen's 40th Anniversary awards. After trading for eight years, sadly it closed in 1999.

Bands

Village orchestras made up of string and reed instruments were often the traditional way of leading the singing in church; such was the case in the Old Meeting House and St Peter's Church where musicians played from the gallery. Whether these same musicians were members of the first Tadley Band we do not know, but in 1875 eight musicians from the Old Meeting House and the Methodist Chapel came together to form the The Tadley Gospel Temperance Band. Because of its formation from nonconformist origins, which in the 19th century took the lead in renouncing alcoholic drink, the name Temperance was undoubtedly a connection to the Temperance movement of that time. Its aim; to provide an alternative, worthwhile recreation to hard drinking.

In 1898 a Salvation Army Corps was established in Tadley and with it the formation of another band. In the early years activities for both bands were confined to religious playing. After a six day working week the musicians often walked miles, few able to afford a bicycle, to attend practices, Hospital Sunday parades (see page 111), open-air services or camp meetings. Such was their enthusiasm. The quality of music might have been short of to-day's standards but it was robust and merry and the only pleasure of its day.

For the Tadley Band, after World War I, alongside its religious activities came the brass band competitions. In 1923, at a cost of £346, gleaming new silver instruments replaced the brass ones and local people now listened to the Tadley Silver Band. How, you might ask, does a silver band compete in a brass band competition? By definition, a brass band contains no wood-wind instruments neither does a silver band. A number of young musicians joined during World War II resulting in the formation of a youth band, now known as Tadley Concert Brass. Under a succession of able trainers in the post war years the band became more competitive, winning many notable trophies. This chapter records just a few of their many successes. Playing an active part in the events of the community was, and still is, high on their agenda. In the early years they often played in Basingstoke's War Memorial Park on a Sunday. Remembrance Day Services, Fêtes and Concerts are still regular engagements.

In the 21st century ther are still two bands. Tadley Silver Band, sponsored by Martin Grant Homes, is now known as Tadley Band (MGH) and Tadley Concert Brass, supported by the training band, who still rely on public support for their funds. Justly proud of their long tradition, which is probably only equalled amongst the brass bands of the factories and collieries of the north, Tadley Bands continue as they began – providing their members with worthwhile recreation and the public with popular entertainment.

↑ Margaret Lane (née West) was the first lady member of Tadley Band. She joined in 1942 and continued a family tradition begun in the 19th century by her grandfather, Gideon, who was an original member of Tadley Salvation Army Band.

↑ The Salvation Army Drum and the confirmed identity of several members of this group (about 1920), would lead to the belief that it was primarily the Salvation Army Band. Together with other Tadley musicians, they have come together to play for the Festive Season. See page 143 for names.

→ Probably one of the earliest photographs of The Gospel Temperance Band with families, taken in 1901. In the background is the cottage which stood between The Primitive Methodist Chapel (page 62) and the road prior to the cottage's demolition.

→ The Salvation Army Band in full strength. It has not been possible to positively identify any member of the group. However, could the 2 ladies, centre front, be Captain Edith Griffin and Lieutenant Alice Inham who, in 1898, arrived in Tadley from London to form the corps?

↑ (top) The band smartly attired in their first uniform of navy with light blue. Under the leadership of David Norris, they entered their first competition in Newbury on 3 August 1914, the day before war was declared. The adjudicator noted 'Here is a band of promise'.

↑ (bottom) A charity fund-raising event for the Royal Berkshire Hospital in the days before the National Health Service (see page 111). This 1922 Hospital Sunday parade shows the Tadley Band marching along a dusty Baughurst road.

↑ Armistice Sunday 1930 at Mortimer. Lady Haig, wife of General Haig, President of the British legion, is seen thanking band master John Lambden for the band's services during the parade and remembrance service.

← John Lambden was appointed band master in 1921, succeeding David Norris. 'Johnnie' was greatly respected and liked. He served the Tadley Band for 25 years before he died suddenly on Good Friday 1946 – a double blow for the band following so closely on the death, in 1945, of Joseph Dyson, the band's professional coach since 1930.

↑ By 1937 the band, now the Tadley Silver Prize Band, were firmly established as competitors in Brass Band competition. This photograph was taken after winning the First and Challenge Shield and Vase at Reading (for names, see page 143). Many individual medals were also awarded. The band were re-equipped with a new uniform this year at a cost of £140. An appeal was made by Ernie Kimber (Hon Secretary) for donations toward the cost.

Among this group are the two young musicians who lost their lives in World War II: Brian West and Stanley Bowman (see page 114).

← Seen here is Flight Sergeant Brian West RAF as a young bandsman. Sadly he was shot down over enemy territory whilst engaged in bombing operations.

© *Reading Chronicle*

↑ A big day for the Tadley Band. Their first ever National contest victory in 1962. After gaining 191 points out of a possible 200 they were presented with the Daily Herald National Challenge Vase and £50. Conductor Gideon West was presented with a bound copy of the score and the baton of honour. Back row (l to r): Adam Brown, Howard Flitters, Fred Hutchins, Stuart Renshaw, Bernard Stone, Victor West, Donald West; front row: Gideon West, Hazel Carter, Ray Lambden.

← In the same year, at Reading Town Hall, Ernie Kimber (photographed) and Gideon West each received Honorary life membership of the Brass Band Club in recognition of 50 years service to the movement. The presentation was made by Harry Mortimer OBE.

© Trinity Mirror plc

↑ 'Following in fathers footsteps' aptly describes the family tradition of band playing in Tadley – a 1959 family group (l to r) William 'Dickie' West and son Brian, Fred Hutchins and in front daughter Ann, (behind) Bernard Stone and son Colin, Victor West with father Ernie, Robert West (third generation bandsman) with father Gideon.

← 1973 Veteran band members, each with over 50 years service; left to right: Jim Tappern, Percy Appleton, Frank Moslin, Arthur Smith, Ernie Kimber. Note the crossed besom broom logo on their blazers.

The loss of so many bandsmen (16) to HM.Forces in World War II led to the encouragement of junior groups of musicians to fill the gap. In 1975 the Youth Band was established with 30 members aged 9-17 years. To-day it is known as Tadley Concert Brass and is under the direction of Paul Chapman, himself a member of the first youth band.

↑ Standing: Ernie Kimber (tutor); seated (l to r) Margaret West (1st female member), Robert West, Brian West, ? James, Eric Rose.

← 1958 Junior Band. Back (l to r): George Dicker, Gideon West, Colin Stone, Jeff Andrews, Bruce Carter, Fred Hutchins, Howard Flitters; seated: Hazel Carter, Ann Hutchins, Marlene Corvey, Janet Chapman, Shirley Sandford, Sylvia Stacey; front: Bill Chapman.

Church and chapel

A short walk around Tadley reveals, through the number of churches and chapels, how important religion has been in the town from early times to the present day. Methodist, Anglican, Salvation Army, Catholic, and United Reformed (Old Meeting), are all represented by their place of worship. In the past people were often identified by their religion, they could be 'chapel people', 'great church goers' or 'members of the Old Meeting'. Whatever the strength of their religious belief, most Tadley people have, over the years, turned to the church to celebrate the main events of their life: getting married, christening their children, and making a last journey along the track at the side of Gravelly Close to St Peter's Church. This track was maintained at a regulation six-foot width, enough room for a horse to pull a hearse or bearers to carry a coffin.

Not only have the churches served the spiritual needs of the community but they also provided education, social activities and entertainment. Many children in the past received their education in Sunday Schools, and at a time when entertainment was limited, an inspiring sermon or a chapel trip to the seaside could be the highlight of comparatively simple lives. Also, as can be seen in chapter four, the Tadley Band has religious origins.

Religion also followed Tadley people to the hop fields. Albert West remembers being impressed by a religious magic lantern show put on by Church Army 'missionaries' where images of Christ were projected onto a bed sheet used as a screen.

In recent years, with education provided by the State, other forms of entertainment and changing lifestyles, the role of the church has become limited in many peoples' lives. Nevertheless, as Tadley's population rose in the post-war years, new churches were built to serve the needs of the community. The photographs on pages 60 and 64 show that at first these places of worship were often redundant wartime buildings.

Although the churches and chapels of Tadley are possibly less full today than in years gone by, they remain to minister in times of need as they have always done. To stand in the grounds of St Peter's Church, or the Old Meeting, is to stand where countless others have stood in joy, pain and sadness down the years. It is also to appreciate how these old churches, and the new, have given help and support to the people of Tadley when they most needed it.

↑ The Revd A S Outhwaite, Vicar of St Mary's Church, wearing new vestments, presented to him at a harvest thanksgiving service in the 1960s. They were made by (l to r) Mrs Cynthia Lisney, Mrs Doreen Cushine and Mrs Sheila Ellis.

2306 Old Church, Tadley.

↑ A pre-1920 photograph of St Peter's Church which is a Grade I listed building. The nave is probably the oldest part, dating from the 13th century, the tower being added in 1685. Originally the tower had a boarded roof which was replaced by tiles in 1879. The brick porch and dormer window over it date from 1689. The remainder of the church is a mix of periods and styles, mainly 17th century.

← An interior view showing the 'Puritan' pulpit with its Jacobean style canopy. The door of the pulpit bears the date 1650. The clearly visible lectern commemorates the end of war in 1945.

← A view of the west end showing the 'facing' gallery dating from the 17th century rebuilding. The Instrumental Choir played here until 1876; instruments played included piccolo, flute, violin, double bass, bass violin, flageolet (type of recorder), haut boy (archaic word for an oboe) and serpent (obsolete wind instrument resembling a snake in shape).

S. SAVIOUR'S CHURCH & RECTORY TADLEY

2310 The Rectory, Tadley

↑ (top) A photograph showing the mission church of St Saviours, with the Rectory on the right and The Green in the foreground. The church stood where 1 Rectory Close is now. Dedicated in 1888, it was demolished some 78 years later following the building of St Paul's Church.

↑ (bottom) The old Rectory viewed from the south. The entrance to the 'Iron Room' can clearly be seen on the right. Situated behind St Saviours, the 'Iron Room' was used for recreational purposes and as a surgery by the local doctors.

↑ (top) A photograph of the
St Saviours Church Choir taken around
1936-37. Back row (l to r): Ted Stroud,
Alec Milne, Geoffrey Gladman, George
(Joe) Cove; front row: Arthur Cubitt,
Gordon Martin, Arthur Cook, Arthur
Miles, Len Cottrell, Ted Upton.

↑ (bottom) A reunion photograph
taken at St Peters Church in 1987.
The missing members are Ted Stroud
deceased and Geoffrey Gladman.

In the mid-1960s St Saviour's was replaced by a new church – St Paul's. St Saviour's was demolished and Rectory Close houses built where it once stood. St Paul's, a new rectory and church hall were all built in the grounds.

← A picture showing the construction of St Paul's Church bell tower. The foundation stone was laid in May 1965 and the church was consecrated a year later.

→ The rector, the Revd Kenneth Davis is seen here dedicating the new bell given by John Stacey. It was cast from four bells removed from Basingstoke Town Hall and weighs 254kg.

↑ Little St Mary's, Heath End Road, was a 'mission church' of St Peter's Church, built in 1874-75. Although Heath End was only a small parish, in its later years the church attracted good congregations, especially during the building of Great St Mary's Church, North Tadley. It finally closed in February 1977 and is now a private dwelling, with the bell tower removed.

→ An interior view showing the altar and pulpit. Note the small oil lamp to the left of the window. Volunteers restored the inside during 1958-59 and electric light and heating were installed. The writing under the window reads, *This do in remembrance of me* referring to the taking of Communion.

TY.5F ST. MARY'S CHURCH, TADLEY

Courtesy The Francis Frith Collection, www.francisfrith.co.uk

The growth in population of north Tadley following the building of AWRE made it necessary to build a central, larger Anglican church.

↑ A photograph of Great St Mary's Church in, appropriately, Newchurch Road, taken in the 1960s. The church was consecrated in June 1961. The buildings on the left have all been demolished and the site is now occupied by the Tadley Telephone Exchange and the Royal Mail Delivery Office.

← One of two Aldermaston Airfield huts, 600 and 601 (see page 104), situated side by side and used in the late 1950s as a temporary church and church hall. They were demolished in March 1960 to clear the site for the commencement in May of Great St Mary's Church. The houses in the background are 59 to 69 Bishopswood Road.

← An internal view of the temporary church showing the screen around the altar and the altar itself with its cross. The pulpit is just visible on the left.

As a result of the Puritan Ejection in 1662 dissenting worshippers abandoned the Church of England, St Peter's, and established an Independent Church, now known as the United Reformed Church.

↑ The Old Meeting House was built in 1718-19. It was enlarged in 1828 and the first day school in Tadley was opened there. Further restoration work was carried out in the 1960s. A Grade II listed building, the exterior has not changed much from this picture – the roof window has been removed and a gabled porch and boundary wall have been added. The adjacent churchyard, one of only two in the town, is where generations of Tadley families are buried.

→ An interior view showing the distinctive gallery, a feature often to be found in non-conformist churches. The pulpit on the left dates from the 1828 addition. The large columns and ceiling beam clearly indicate the division betwen the old and new areas.

In the early 19th century the Methodist movement split into several groups, many supporters believing that it had lost much of its original fervour. As a result, the Primitive Methodist Society was formed in 1810.

↑ A 1905 Primitive Methodist Sunday School outing. It would probably have been to somewhere fairly local, possibly the common.

→ The Primitive Methodist Chapel, situated in Main Road, Tadley. Erected in 1859, it was used for worship until the adjacent new Methodist Chapel was built in 1931. The building was sold in 1986 and has since been converted into a private dwelling.

→ Sunday School group at the Primitive Methodist Chapel in 1923. Amongst the group are members of the Kimber family, Florrie Englefield and Polly West.

↑ (top) An interior view of Main Road Methodist Church shortly after it opened in 1931. The Lord's table and pulpit are clearly visible as are the stylish oil lamps, there being no electricity in the church at the time.

↑ (bottom) An exterior view of the church. In recent times it has undergone a major refurbishment with the porch in the picture being removed and replaced by a white rendered panel with a black cross. A back addition has been built creating a new entrance and hallway. The pulpit's position was changed and is now at the east or Main Road end.

The newly formed community of north Tadley in the 1950s found themselves remote from the Methodist Church in Main Road and so met on 2 July 1956 to establish a new Methodist Church.

↑ Hut 227, one of the old Aldermaston Airfield buildings, was used as Tadley Common Methodist Church in the late 1950s, prior to the construction of the new church.

→ The stone laying ceremony for the new Methodist Church held on Saturday 5 September 1959. The houses at the top of the photograph are in Huntsmoor Road.

→ Tadley Common Methodist Church, Newchurch Road, was consecrated in September 1960. Pastor Stanley Belcher led the congregation until the appointment of the first minister, Revd Alfred Olds, in 1962.

Courtesy The Francis Frith Collection, www.francisfrith.co.uk

↑ (top) St Michael's Catholic Church, Bishopswood Road. A chapel-cum-hall was opened in 1959 and at that time Father Michael Young served the spiritual needs of the community from Douai Abbey. In 1962 the Diocese took over responsibility for the church and Father Desmond O'Ryan became the first parish priest.

↑ (bottom) Taken in 1969, this picture shows a group of First Communicants outside the church. The priest is Father O'Ryan, the lady on the left is Eileen O'Donovan and the lady on the right is Jane Harden.

Salvation Army Hall. Tadley.

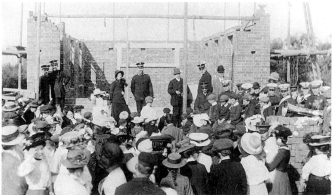

↑ The Salvation Army first came to Tadley in 1898 but this hall was not built until 1909 by Noah Blake. Over the years it has had many extensions, the most recent in 2001; the one in 1955 was opened by Lady Mount.

← The foundation stone laying ceremony for the new hall in 1907. Notice the Salvation Army band, formed in the 19th century, on the right. Preachers at the hall have included William Booth.

← An early 1920s photograph of Noah and Emily Blake on their Golden Wedding day. The photograph was taken at their home in the lane now bearing the family name – Blakes Lane. Back row (l to r) Noah Jnr, Bert (not Albert), Albert, Frederick 'Fred', George, Harry. Front row: Rose, Emily, Noah, William 'Bill' and Polly. Missing from the celebrations were two sisters, Bessie and Florence, who lived in Canada.

↑ (top) A photograph showing carter, Charlie West, with visitors to a Salvation Army meeting whom he had collected from Aldermaston Station. The young boy in the the cart is Alfred Aldridge. Mrs Lily Stacey remembers the cart also being used for Salvation Army outings and picnics.

↑ (bottom) The Young Persons' Singing Company of 1926-27. Back row (l to r): Maisie West, Connie Englefield née Stamp, Alice Lambden, Annie Bowman, Nellie Nash, Edie West née Pearce, Elsie Lambden, Violet West; middle row: Francis Lambden, Nellie Appleton née Moss, Lt Arthur Smith, Captain Harold Smith (no relation), Lily Stacey née Moss, Nellie Moss née Savage; front row: Cyril Chapman, Frank(ie) Moss.

Trade and commerce

As the population of the area has grown and social and economic developments have taken place, so opportunities for expanding trade and commerce in Tadley have been grasped by local entrepreneurs. If there has been a theme to this expansion it is that a significant part has been linked to travel and transport. From the sale and repair of bicycles in modest premises, or the carter taking out local products and bringing back ordered items, to the fleet of lorries and heavy plant of Brants and John Stacey & Sons, the need to transport people and materials has been important to local commerce. As traffic along the A340 increased more businesses were established to meet demand. The first garage, run by Ambrose Allen, was followed later by Whatmores, The Falcon, and Esso garages, and in 1956 Peg's Cafe opened to serve refreshments to motorists and workers.

The increase in population and affluence has reversed the way local trade and commerce often operated. Instead of local bakers, butchers and carriers bringing goods to people in small scattered communities like Tadley, by horse-drawn cart and later vans, we now travel to the supermarket or towns by car. However even in the late 1960s Whatmore's supermarket would deliver any shopping to your home for a charge of 6d.

This chapter also records the changing fortunes of local businesses. Some of them relatively short-lived like Bargains Galore, others like John Stacey & Sons can trace their origins back to 1871. Some older residents are reluctant to let go of companies which they have dealt with for many years; referring to Budgens as Whatmores, because for over thirty years from 1945 that was the name of the shop that occupied the prominent position on Mulfords Hill. Apart from name changes several shops are still immediately recognisable today: Mulfords Hill parade on page 80, Jewell's on page 75, Whatmore's garage on page 78, but it is hard to relate the patch of scrub land along Tadley Hill to the substantial butcher's shop shown on page 70. Newer businesses in Tadley, like elsewhere, are often indicative of social change. In the post-war years the only take-away was Tom Stacey's fish and chip shop, now there is an Indian restaurant and a range of international take-away food shops in the town.

Trade and commerce in Tadley has had to modernise or adapt to survive and as can be seen in this chapter it has often resulted in the expansion and conversion of premises. This is a process that still continues today and the nature of future commercial developments will have an important impact on the sort of place Tadley will become in future years.

↑ George Middleton, local butcher in the early 1920s, trading from his Trojan delivery van.

↑ (top) Barn Close Laundry, Church Road. A very early 20th century photograph of employees smartly attired in their uniforms. It is believed that many young women came from homes for orphans, certainly none have been identified. By 1923 the laundry had closed.

↑ (bottom) The Old Malthouse, Malthouse Lane in about 1908. By this date it is no longer a small scale family maltings but part of the Farnham United Breweries Ltd selling and delivering Fine Ales and Stouts. Pictured are W Stacey (proprieter), J Chapple and D Chandler.

↑ W Barker, family butchers, on Tadley Hill in about 1934. The business was probably started by Frederick Hussey. By the time this photograph was taken it had been bought by Ansteys of Reading. Notice the various carcasses hung outside and two delivery vans indicating a wide catchment area of customers. Among the group of employees is Frank Saunders (second from left).

← The most well know local Hussey's butcher's shop was in New Road. Tommy Marks bought the business after World War II, eventually selling it to Brian Gooch – seen here on the right in the 1980s with his assistant Fred Morley.

← The butcher's shop closed in October 1988 and the premises were converted into the Morland Surgery.

↑ James' blacksmith's forge, Pamber Heath Road, in the 1930s. With the decline in the need for smithing Stan diversified, selling and repairing cycles and running a taxi service. Pictured outside the shop adjoining the smithy, is Les Ward (right) with ?.

→ Edward 'Ted' Hutchins' business on Mulfords Hill is now the site of a greengrocers and music shop (Tadley Instruments). In the photograph is his son Fred who after World War II ran the business mainly as a cycle shop.

→ A photograph from about 1925 with the Kimbers Bakery (Pamber End) delivery van parked outside The Hawthorns (now demolished) on The Green. In front of the Ford Model T van is driver Arthur Martin, son of the landlord of The Fighting Cocks public house (see page 35).

↑ A photograph from about 1925 of a Reading to Tadley Thames Valley bus with (left) driver 'Sid' Englefield and (right) conductor Frank Wickens Senior. This was an ex-War Department Thorneycroft J-type lorry with solid tyres to which was fitted a 54 seater body. Behind is a steam wagon.

← An earlier photograph (about 1914) of Bill Lay(e) (right) and William Kent (left) with his original grey painted carriers van, a 28–32 hp Daimler. He ran a daily carrier service (except Thursday and Sunday) to Basingstoke via Baughurst, Tadley, Pamber and Sherborne St John. The occasional passenger was often taken in addition to parcels, provisions and livestock.

← A line-up of William Kent's coach fleet outside their Baughurst garage in about 1933. In the foreground is the 'pride of the fleet', a Morris Commercial Viceroy (CG 675) which was purchased at the 1932 Motor Show.

↑ A 1925 photograph of Ambrose Allen with his dog standing in front of his first car, a Daimler, which he used as a taxi. Beside Ambrose is Arthur Martin who worked for him for 28 years before joining Webbers of Basingstoke.

← Allen's Garage, Tadley Hill during the 1950s. The photograph shows the original World War I ex-army hut it was housed in. The small building to the left was used by 'Gussi', Ambrose Allen's sister, to sell 'antiques'. In 1924 Thames Valley Transport extended its bus service between Reading and Tadley (see page 72). The buses, a single and a double decker, were stored overnight in the large shed that is to the right of the garage.

↑ (top) This view of Stacey's shop on Tadley Hill, taken in 1922, shows Sarah Ann (mother of Florrie and Tom) Stacey outside the family fruiterer's and fishmonger's business. At this time it was not the village post office, which was still located opposite the Methodist Church (see page 63).

↑ (bottom left) A rare interior view of a village shop in 1947. Note the jars and boxes of sweets on prominent display – enticing passing schoolchildren to spend their pocket money!

↑ (bottom right) Keri and Florrie Evans pictured outside Tadley Hill Post Office which they kept for many years. Although Tom Stacey was the registered Postmaster it was his sister, Florrie, who ran the post office while Tom kept the adjoining fish shop and mobile van service. The shop and Post Office closed in January 1995.

© Rural History Centre, The University of Reading

↑ (top) Irwin Jewell originally had a mobile shop. In 1951 the construction of AWRE increased business and he erected a wooden hut in Franklin Avenue as a general store. This 1957-58 photograph shows on the left Mary Mawson and Diana Molloy (née Orchard). In 1959 it became Richardson & Rabbetts newsagents, then a record shop and latterly a bakery – The Chelsea Bun, now closed.

↑ (bottom) A late 1950s photograph of the Englefield family home in Franklin Avenue. It became the site of two family businesses: Ted's barber shop and Eileen's Taxi service (1974-84). The property has been considerably extended and renamed Emit House, but Ted's barber shop still occupies the side extension.

↑ A photograph from about 1915 of Blake's village shop, the forerunner of the present supermarket on Mulfords Hill. Built by 'Albie' (Albert) Blake senior as a shop for his wife Dorothy to run. During World War I, while Albert was away, she brought up their family and ran the shop single handed.

← View looking north along Mulfords Hill with Pilgrim's Cottage on the right. Behind it is Whatmore's shop with an early extension to the original Blake's shop. Between 1945 and 1963 there were 16 extensions, increasing the shop frontage to 28 metres.

← A mid-1960s view of Whatmore's delivery vans, lined up in front of the shop. Their first van (KCG 773) is the Trojan in the centre; on the left is a Morris J2 (KHO 790) and on the right, a Thames model (TOR 858), which was new in 1958. Notice the pharmacy is now part of the complex.

In addition to the food department, Whatmore's, like its modern counterparts, also sold wines, spirits, flowers and stationery. The store's proud claim was that a customer could buy almost anything they required from a washing machine or lawn mower to toys or drapery. In addition there was a travel agency and pharmacy.

↑ (top) Staff and customers pose for a photograph featured in the *Self-service & Supermarket Journal,* September 1963.

↑ (bottom) Due to the considerable growth of the business the store was converted to self-service in September 1961. By September 1963 Whatmore's employed 54 staff.

↑ Whatmore's Garage (now Wheelgame) occupied the site of Pilgrim's Cottage, south of Whatmore's supermarket on Mulfords Hill. This photograph shows the early stages of its construction with a temporary hut in use to ensure the continuation of business. Bernard Judd, standing beside the petrol pumps, later became the co-owner of Bernard's DIY store.

← Opening day of the new garage. The tall hedge in the top photograph has been removed to reveal the adjacent cottage. The site is now occupied by Unwins, Tulipa and Husseys.

← Mr J S Whatmore (centre) viewing a Morris Mini which was on loan from Webber's Garage, Basingstoke. For a short period during the 1960s Whatmores included car sales amongst their many retail ventures.

↑ (top and bottom) Bargains Galore was a real aladdin's cave, selling everything from bottled gas to buttons, wool to birthday cards. The shop, which opened in 1973, was located off the A340 – down the path beside the library which at the time linked Mulfords Hill to the Silchester Road through Stacey's Yard. The premises were leased from John Stacey but the business was owned by Jean Webb who ran it with the help of her daughters, Angela and Donna. It finally closed in 1988.

↑ (top) The Mulfords Hill parade of shops has changed little since the late 1950s when this photograph was taken; (l to r) police house, Jobs Dairy (now Estate Agents), E D Eyles's greengrocer (take-away), Beryl Weston's haberdashery (bank) Bernards Ironmongers (Kings DIY).

↑ (bottom) Kathleen and Douglas Eyles ran their greengrocery and florist shop on the Mulfords Hill parade for thirty years between 1958-88. The site is now a take-away.

↑ (top) A mid-1960s photograph of Barclay's Bank in Aldermaston Road which was built in 1952. It has since been redeveloped into a larger two storey building. The Boundary Hall hostel in the background has now been demolished (see pages 105 and 130).

↑ (bottom) Between 1907-20 Tadley Post Office was situated on the east side of Main Road. It was run from the single storey extension to the house which is now known as The Hawthorns. Mrs Alice Whitehorne was the appointed sub-postmistress at that time. The house is now a private dwelling.

The name of John Stacey is well known throughout the south as a demolition and plant hire company with offices at Whitehouse Farm, Silchester Road and in Sussex. John and Lily Stacey began the business with just one lorry, after the closure of the brick kiln at the beginning of World War II.

↑ A photograph from about 1949 showing one of J Stacey's early lorries, a 4-6 ton Bedford, with driver Archie Pike.

← George Henry Stacey and wife Martha, celebrating their golden wedding anniversary in 1959. They were the parents of John who began the haulage business in 1939-40. George and Martha lived at The Green from 1936. He donated the land for the building of the Memorial Hall.

↑ Peg's Cafe, built in 1956, was situated on the Aldermaston Road, where the Falcon Fields estate stands today. Denis Brant and his mother started the venture, then his sister Peggy took over. Denis expanded his own business as a garden and estate contractor into a thriving haulage and demolition contracting company – D Brant Ltd. Often his employees would have a hearty breakfast in the cafe before commencing their day's work.

← An interesting photograph showing the inside of the cafe with Denis and Peggy ready for the customers. The premises closed in 1984 when the site was redeveloped as Falcon Fields.

← One of the familiar fleet of yellow and red vehicles belonging to D Brant Ltd. involved in demolition and clearance work.

Working life

During the 19th and for much of the first part of the 20th century the world was, quite literally, a world of work for most Tadley people. They lived in small, scattered cottages where the home was the workplace or the workplace was a short walk away. Their lives centred on work; when they were not making besom brooms, the men were working in their allotments or gardens. Women also found jobs like stripping willow osiers or helping with the process of making brooms, as well as bringing up children and managing the home – often on slender means.

Up until World War II it was the woodland crafts that often provided a basic living, with besom broom-making the mainstay of most family incomes. However, it was a seasonal job and in order to supplement their income, men often had to travel outside Tadley for work. In spring they picked bark for the leather tanning industry, sometimes as far away as Sussex, in summer they sought work on farms and in early autumn whole families decamped to the hop fields around Alton. Being able to turn their hand to various occupations often helped to relieve some of the poverty and hardship for people. Charlie West for example, seen on page 67, started a smallholding, made a few besom brooms when time permitted, and had in the past operated an occasional carting service, collecting travellers from Aldermaston station and bringing them to Tadley.

Regular employment in agriculture has not been a major feature of life in Tadley. There were several farms in the village – Church Brook Farm is the only one left – but apart from the owners they only provided work for a few people. Some people found work in the brickworks or as servants in the larger houses, but in the main most people were independent workers.

After World War II economic conditions changed, enabling local entrepreneurs to flourish. New skills were needed and new jobs were created, such as mechanics for the post-war garages as they catered for the expanding car owning population. Dennis Brant and John Stacey became important local employers and their vehicles were a common sight in the area. Obviously though the major impact on employment in Tadley was the opening in 1950 of the Atomic Weapons Research Establishment. With its development came a massive expansion of population and career opportunities.

Today, the opportunities for employment in Tadley are more varied. However, despite computers, supermarkets, nuclear weapons and all the modern changes of recent years, besom brooms continue to be made in Tadley as they have been since probably the 16th century, and now 'By Royal Appointment'!

↑ Frederick Cove and his wife at Pound Farm, Church Road. They farmed there in the period between World War I and World War II.

The long history of besom broom-making in Tadley probably reached its peak during the 100 years prior to World War II.

↑ George West's broom yard, Mulfords Hill (approximately where Gorselands is today – see page 22). This photograph, taken about 1910, clearly shows the stages in besom broom production. From right to left: faggots (bavins) stacked ready for stripping, probably by the lady sitting nearby at the shaving-horse; binding twigs for the broom head; using a draw-shave to form a handle; fixing a handle and to the rear the pile of completed brooms. Among the group are Eli West (far right) Daniel West (in suit) and George West (shaving handle).

← Of the many thousands of brooms made, many came from an individual working alone at his cottage, often in the place where father and grandfather before him had plied the same trade.

© *Rural History Centre, The University of Reading*

↑ A 1920s photograph of the Bowman family at their broomyard in Sandy Lane. Left to right: Sylvanus Pike (visiting), Fred Bowman (Junior), Fred Bowman (father of Fred and Alf) with Mickey the dog and Alf Bowman.

← Alfred West at his yard on Mulfords Hill (approximately Hillcrest). This was the last of the old broom yards to close when Alfred retired in 1950. A prolific yard at its busiest, Billy 'Stumpy' West and son Alfred employed in excess of seven workers and could produce over 80,000 brooms a year.

← The Lane, Mulfords Hill. Joe Savage binding twigs for a broom head.

© *Rural History Centre, The University of Reading*

↑ (top) A photograph from about 1907 of Tommy Saunders' broomyard in Broadhalfpenny Lane. In the background is the tell-tale sign of the broom maker's trade – a great pile of birch faggots (bavins) neatly built into a rick. The birch is left to season for several months until hard and pliable.

↑ (bottom) Local woodland also supplied craftsmen such as Mr S Cox of Mulfords Hill with hazel coppice for hurdle making; a 1958 photograph.

Situated in the centre of the woodland district of north Hampshire, Tadley was ideally positioned to benefit from the 19th century growth in demand for woodland products. Following the sale of 'standing' wood at auction in November, wood dealers employed local woodmen to fell the timber.

↑ (top) A group of Tadley men in their bivouac. Woodmen often travelled long distances sleeping rough in lean-to shelters, moving from wood to wood felling and sorting.

↑ (bottom) A pre-1914 photograph of a local tree felling gang. After World War I they came together again as a gang. Most of the group were related and on Saturday mornings younger members of their respective families were taken on the backs of motorcycles to help by making tea, clearing branches etc. Left to right: ?, Peter Wigley, ?, ?, ?, David (Leslie) Englefield (see page 115). Two of the 'unknowns' are believed to be William Englefield, brother of David, and Alfred Smith.

↑ Bark stripping was another seasonal woodland occupation. Oak bark was used for the tanning of leather. Some bark stripping was carried out locally but most Tadley men travelled throughout southern England to work. A pre-1914 photograph showing, back row (l to r): Job West, Gideon West, ?, ?; front row: Israel West, ?, ?, Walter Aldridge, Albert 'Lively' West.

← A more unusual job for Tadley men – directors and work force, in about 1899, during archaeological excavations at Roman Silchester. Back row (l to r): Bill Benham, George West, ?, ? Smith, Eli Smith, ? Smith; front row: ? Butler, Arthur Monger, ?, ?, Charles Lambden (?), ?, ?.

From Victorian times until the 1940s, hop picking for the brewing industry was a common seasonal occupation for local people. Tadley families would spend between three and four weeks in September hop-picking in the Alton area – working five and a half days a week,

finishing at Saturday lunchtime. Mechanisation and competition from imported foreign hops killed off the need for seasonal labour in the 1960s.

↑ This photograph, taken in about 1928 at Coldrey Farm near Bentley, shows (l to r)

Percy West, Elsie West (later Simpson) with their mother Ruth West filling their basket with hops. A family such as the Wests might pick up to 80 bushels (80 baskets) a day at 2d (1p) a bushel – a good wage for a month's work.

Hop picking was looked upon as something of an adventure for those who enjoyed it. The working season in the hop fields was also a holiday for many.

↑ Photograph shows a 'visiting' day at a Bentley hop farm. Some came via transport while others biked or walked considerable distances. The accommodation barracks in the background consisted of a partitioned section per family. In the early years a rough blanket spread on straw made a bed while cooking was done outside. Identified faces in the group are believed to include: Walt Saunders, Lena Chapman, Elsie Trusler, Bill Savage, Nellie Moss, Dolly Nash, Ern Nash, Mrs Fred Chapman, Libby Chapman, Sue Savage, Arthur Cottrell, Frances Lambden, Nellie Lambden, Arthur Moss.

← A 1950s photograph with Ruth West (left) and Elizabeth West (not related), mother of Albert West (see page 97) picking hops.

↑ (top) The range of seasonal work locals undertook in the past was broad. This photograph from the 1920s or 1930s shows a more out of the ordinary seasonal job for Tadley men: potato pickers off to the Channel Islands.

↑ (bottom) Regular employment in agriculture was not a common feature of Tadley life, but photographed here is George 'Curly' Saunders (see page 123) working in his father's (Alfie) field at Pamber Green, now Greenacres Garden Centre. Taken in the 1920s, in the background can be seen buildings on the Basingstoke to Tadley road (A340).

↑ (top) Bishopswood Golf Course has now replaced this farmland. The clubhouse stands on the site of the old farm buildings and house that was owned and farmed by the Appleton family.

↑ (bottom left) Albert Appleton and his wife Kate née Hawkins. Albert is recorded as farmer at Bishopswood throughout the 1920s and early 1930s.

↑ (bottom right) A photograph of Percy Appleton, taken about 1965, before he left Bishopswood Farm. The farm remained empty for a time, following the auction at which it was sold to Blakes the Builders (see page 66).

The production of bricks and tiles became an important local industry with their increased use as a primary building material. There were brickyards at Little London, Ramsdell, Inhurst and Tadley by the late 19th century or before. By 1911 John Stacey senior was the sole owner of the Tadley brickworks site, his son George Henry, the listed brick merchant (see page 82). These two photographs show workers at the site in the early 1900s.

↑ William Nash is seen holding a brick mould. Behind him is a 'bearing off' barrow part loaded with shaped bricks ready for firing. Notice the upturned hurdle behind the bench acting as a crude shelter.

← Believed to be Stephen Boyd/ West. Here we see the fired bricks still stacked awaiting removal on the 'crowding' barrow.

The stripping of willow osiers for weaving into cradles, fish traps etc, and most importantly during World War I for ammunition baskets, was mainly carried out at the western end of the parish, Heath End: ie Brown's yard at Wigmore Heath, Shyshack Lane, and Sylvanus and Jane Hick's yard next to Little St Mary's Church, Heath End Road.

↑ A photograph from around 1910. The aprons would indicate it was a working day at this rod yard, but many of the hats would not look out of place at Ascot! Among the group are members of the Savage family.

← Tom Sandford of Shyshack Lane, stripping bark from willow by hand – a job usually done with a 'brake'.

Houses and buildings

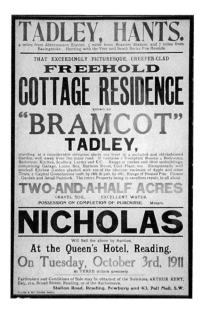

In his great survey of all the buildings of architectural importance in England, Nikolaus Pevsner found little in Tadley that impressed him. Only St Peter's Church and the 'Elizabethan stone chimneypiece' of Tadley Place are recorded in the Hampshire volume. It may be true that Tadley lacks buildings of national importance, but there are sixteen listed buildings and two Conservation areas in the town. The photographs included in this chapter of The Wilderness, Heath End House, and Hawley House, show how splendid the houses of local gentry were in their prime. These houses of the well-to-do are of a relatively recent date; only Tadley Place dates from before the 19th century, indicating that for much of its history Tadley was mainly the home of the so-called labouring classes.

The amorphous nature of Tadley clearly indicates that the early village was not developed to an overall plan. It was not an estate village or one that grew around a village green. The inhabitants put up their simple homes close to their place of trade or near the source of their raw material, on whatever land they could afford and where the geological conditions were suitable. Some built where they could, by claiming squatters rights and fencing off waste land. The early homes of these 'labouring classes' were often insubstantial and many have been destroyed by neglect and the elements. The photograph of Mothe's House shortly before it was demolished illustrates this process. More have been reduced to rubble by the developers' bulldozers.

Some of the photographs on the following pages show the transitory and makeshift buildings utilised in Tadley while it, like the rest of Britain, recovered from World War II. Redundant army Nissen huts and railway carriages became temporary homes in the post-war housing shortage; the photographs of the library show that it would be many years before it eventually found modern permanent accommodation.

Many of the houses and buildings of old Tadley have for various reasons been destroyed, but much also remains alongside the modern estates: cruck and timber framed homes of yeomen, farmhouses of the rural middle class, and the simple dwellings of the less well-off. It is our responsibility to ensure that they remain to tell in brick, thatch, and wood the story of Tadley, its history and development.

↑ When this property in West Street was sold at auction in 1911 the sale particulars described a much grander property than that which was built in the 17th century.

In recent years many of the old traditional Tadley dwellings have disappeared. 13 West Street, known locally simply as 'Alberts' is a unique one room dwelling that still remains.

↑ The unmarried brothers Alfred and Albert West with Timmy the cat, taken in 1992. Sadly Alfred died in 1996.

← Albert's house has altered little over the years – a small single-roomed dwelling with a corrugated roof. Beside the house are the sheds and stocks of raw materials for his broom making business. The building on the right, which has replaced an earlier one, was the main accommodation for Job and Elizabeth West and their eleven children in the early 1900s.

← *A Broom Maker's Cottage*, a prize winning garden at the 2001 Chelsea Flower Show. The brain child of Heath End Gardening Club, the entry was based on old Tadley houses and the traditional besom-making trade.

© English Heritage.NMR

↑ (top) Mothe's House stood on the north side of The Green and was built as the result of a deed given by William Mothe in 1739 to the poor of Tadley rent free. It was demolished in 1966 and replaced with six purpose built flats for the elderly.

↑ (bottom) A photograph from about 1965 of Saunders Cottage, one of a small group of dwellings in The Lane on the west side of Mulfords Hill. It was the home of Ernie, broom-maker, and his wife Lily. The site is now part of Saunders Gardens.

↑ (top) A photograph taken about 1930 of Burrell's Farm, now a Grade II listed building, situated on the west side of Main Road. The cottage is reputed to be over 600 years old and is possibly the oldest house in Tadley. Latterly it was known as Grant's Farm due to a 70-year association with the Grant family. Little alteration was undertaken externally during this period although the door, here shown on the left, is now on the right.

↑ (bottom) This cottage – 2 Winston Avenue – has been extensively altered since this 1960s photograph was taken. In 1963, during building work, the then owner's son, discovered a number of George III gold guineas and half guineas in a box under a pear tree in the garden. A Coroner's jury ruled that the find was not 'treasure trove' so they were handed back to the lucky boy. The house is now known as *Pear Tree Cottage.*

↑ A pre-1908 photograph of Tadley Place showing the 18th century additions to the surviving east wing of the former Tudor manor house. It is situated in Church Road to the south of St Peter's Church (see page 55). In the 19th century it was a working farm. The timber framework no longer shows; it is now covered by a rough cast exterior.

← From 1927 Tadley Place, now a Grade II listed building, has been a private residence. In this view a small window in the left gable end, previously bricked up, has been reopened and Elizabethan style stone-mullioned lattice windows installed.

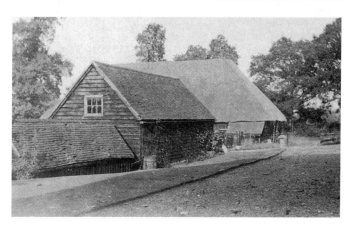

← A photograph of the Tithe barn in the grounds of *Tadley Place*, thought to be one of the largest thatched barns in the county.

↑ A photograph of Hawley House taken in the early 1900s. A Grade II listed building, standing in it own grounds on the corner of Church Road and New Road. A stone in the brickwork reads 'JP 1823' and is thought to be the initials of the builder with the date of its construction. Since about 1915 it has been known as Hawley Farm. The front elevation has changed very little since this picture was taken although now there are no bay windows. In the mid-1920s the Tadley Carnival and Fete were held in the grounds (see pages 40-41).

→ A photograph of George James, a dairy farmer and family, who occupied Hawley Farm for about 60 years. The two ladies standing are his daughters Ethel and Ella, whilst seated are George, his wife Alice and their son William.

↑ Heath End House was situated between Heath End Road and Bishopswood Lane. It is mentioned in the 1861 census as being occupied by John Hobbs, a farmer. However its architectural features are early 20th century. The house was occupied for nearly 40 years by the McConnel family. After William McConnel's death in 1943 the house was commandeered for use first by the Auxiliary Fire Service, followed by the WRNS and the Royal Navy. It was later converted into flats, but in the 1970s it was demolished to make way for the Sheridan Crescent housing development.

© Rural History Centre, The University of Reading

↑ The Wilderness in the early 1920s. Since 1927 it has been known as Tadley Court. When it was put up for public auction in 1920 it was described as 'an exceptionally attractive Gentleman's Country Residence surrounded on all sides by the picturesque and famous Tadley Common'.

← The drawing room with its sliding doors open, showing the ante-room and its open fireplace. The standard lamp indicates that electricity had already been installed by 1920.

← A former owner of the house was Major George Roller, who died in 1941. He is remembered, amongst other things, as being an outstanding soldier, a skilled artist and writer, and an accomplished steeplechase rider.

For several years after the end of World War II the landscape of Tadley was dominated by the old airfield buildings – either being re-used or providing a backdrop to new housing developments.

↑ This photograph taken in the late 1950s from Bishopswood Road shows some of the remaining World War II buildings on Site No 2. The white gable end view, visible on the left, is the old Community Centre (see page 107) and the building in the centre is believed to be part of the 'Chivers Hostel' site (see page 9). The row of houses are in Huntsmoor Road and the huts on the right were used for church purposes prior to the building of Great St Mary's Church (see page 60).

← Pam West and her children Alan and Ann in front of a row of World War II Nissen huts in Blakes Lane. These huts housed 35-40 families and were converted into temporary dwellings by the Rural District Council. The modifications included a kitchen with a Rayburn, toilet, bathroom,

↑ (top) A view taken from the site of Great St Mary's Church (see page 60) and dominated by one of the World War II water towers. The row of houses are in Bishopswood Road and the large building under construction is Burnham Copse Junior School (see page 10), which opened in 1960.

↑ (bottom) A pre-1950 photograph showing the wartime airfield huts known as Instructional Site No 1. It comprised pilots' rest and locker rooms together with facilities for Flight Officers and gunnery crews. The Ministry of Works redeveloped the site to form the Boundary Hall Hostel (see page 130) for AWRE employees. Boundary Hall was demolished in 1995/96.

Hampshire Library Service began in 1924; initially the Tadley area had a mobile service. From the 1950s Berkshire County Council provided a small library for the AWRE housing estates; in 1976 this became a mobile service but closed soon afterwards.

↑ Opened on 27 September 1971, Tadley's second library was a prefabricated building located in Newchurch Road – near where the Community Centre is today.

← Tadley's first library was housed in one of the wartime Aldermaston Airfield buildings: Hut 283, off Bishopswood Road. Rented from the Ministry of Defence, it was opened in 1958.

← The current purpose-built library, adjacent to Mulfords Hill shops, was opened by the Lord Lieutenant of Hampshire, Mrs Mary Fagan, on 12 October 1994. Pictured with her are Councillor Don Allen and Mrs Ruth Hyson, Chair of Hampshire County Council's Recreation Committee.

© Newbury Weekly News (Peter Bloodworth)

↑ (top) The Old Community Centre, Newchurch Road was originally the Aldermaston Airfield gymnasium and chapel (Building 223). It later served as a hostel for the employees of A E Chivers & Sons Ltd during the construction of AWRE, after which it became a centre for community social events.

↑ (bottom left) Left to right: George Beavers, Chairman of Kingsclere & Whitchurch Rural District Council, Ron Latham, Ted Newley, Director of AWRE in 1965 and Revd Outhwaite. Each a prominent member of Tadley & District Community Association. The Beavers and Newley rooms at the new Community Centre are named after two of the above.

↑ (bottom right) Councillor John Shears, Mayor of Basingstoke in the presence of Keith Chapman, Chairman of the Leisure Services Committee, officially opened the new Community Centre on 26 November 1994. He is photographed here being presented with the local emblem, a besom broom.

Healthcare

Before the early 20th century it was rare for ordinary people in rural areas like Tadley to be visited by a doctor, and treatment in a hospital, if available, was often something to be avoided because of the primitive state of medicine. With doctors and hospitals non-existent or expensive, reliance was placed on folk remedies: rubbing a horse to cure whooping cough for example, common sense, quacks, and patent medicine. In 1901 Grimault's Indian cigarettes were being advertised as a cure for asthma! Not surprisingly these remedies were usually ineffective. Nationally, in 1900, one in seven children died before they were one year old compared to the 1992 figure of one in 143. Nearly half of all child deaths under five were caused by whooping cough. The Tadley School log-book regularly records the fear and concern when diseases or 'fevers' affected the area as even everyday complaints like measles and diarrhoea still killed thousands of children each year in the 19th century.

Better diet, improved living conditions, sanitation and a greater access to doctors and hospitals transformed healthcare and local people shared in these advances. In 1902 Dr William Langley opened the first general practice in Tadley which remained until the early 1930s. After this date doctors based in Aldermaston provided local healthcare, until Dr Joe Morland opened a surgery in the grounds of his home, Kiln House, in the early 1950s. He established a continuous practice that would lead to the opening of the purpose-built healthcentres that we have in Tadley today.

Until 1879, and the opening of the Basingstoke Cottage Hospital, the only hospital in the area was the Royal Berkshire Hospital in Reading. Opened in 1839 with only 60 beds it is obvious that, with access so restricted, few Tadley people saw the inside of this hospital. The local workhouse did however provide some basic medical care for those incapable of looking after themselves at home. Following the implementation of the National Health Service in 1948, medical treatment without charge became available to all. As a result the Royal Berkshire Hospital underwent massive expansion. In 1974 the Basingstoke District Hospital eventually replaced the by then inadequate Basingstoke Cottage Hospital in Hackwood Road.

For the people of Tadley today, excellent local medical facilities are freely and easily available to everyone who needs them. The photographs of Hospital Sundays in this chapter record a time when this was not always the case. In the cottages of old Tadley many had to suffer in silence as lack of money, paucity of medical help, and rudimentary healthcare prevented their illnesses being treated.

↑ A young Joe Morland, the much liked and respected local doctor. He came to the Tadley area in 1951, living first in Aldermaston as assistant to Dr Lionel Holmwood and later with Mr and Mrs George Stacey at The Green, Tadley.

In the 19th century Friendly Societies, like the Ancient Order of Foresters, were formed to provide security through mutual self-help from the consequences of accidents, ill health or death.

↑ (top) The Pride of Tadley, branch 7211 of the Ancient Order of Foresters, was formed in 1884. This photograph shows members at an annual Foresters' Day. The drum's badge would indicate that the bandsmen are from the Salvation Army, dating the photograph to post 1898.

↑ (bottom) Leading the march are a group of Tadley Foresters carrying the Court banner. This massive banner had the arms of the Order hand painted on silk. Photograph taken prior to 1914.

Prior to the middle of the 19th century hospitals and places for the treatment of the sick were available primarily only to the rich; for the majority, treatment was administered at home with severe cases admitted to the Workhouse Infirmary where treatment was free.

↑ The Basingstoke Infirmary, Cowdery Down Hospital, was built in 1898. The name was generally dropped in favour of Basing Road Hospital.

← Situated in Hackwood Road, the Cottage Hospital opened in 1878-79 with accommodation for only eight patients!

← The Shrubbery opened as a maternity hospital in 1947 following its sale to Basingstoke Council. This photograph, from about 1910, shows it as a private house – home to the Burberry family between 1909-46.

Prior to the establishment of
The National Health Service in
1948 hospitals were maintained
by voluntary means. Locally,
fundraising was for the Royal
Berkshire Hospital in Reading,
Tadley's nearest large hospital at
the time.

↑ A pause in the day's parade
for people to rest and be
entertained. Among those in
the crowd are Mr and Mrs
Eddie Mead, Daisy West, Rose
West, Matt Ward, Ted Smith
and Revd Ward.

→ The procession gathers
outside The Fox and Hounds,
(see page 36) Mulfords Hill.
A group of bandsmen are
assembled beneath the sign.

→ A view that has changed
little since the 19th century.
The Royal Berkshire Hospital
was officially opened on 27
May 1839. King William IV was
a patron and Richard Benyon
of Englefield House one of the
subscribers.

In 1986 Dr Joe Morland established the first purpose-built surgery in Tadley utilising part of the garden at Kiln House. Prior to this health care in Tadley was spread over a wide area with surgeries held in private houses.

↑ The Goddard home at 46 Mulfords Hill, where the front room was used as a surgery by Dr Lionel Holmwood during World War II. Photograph taken on Christmas Day 1940.

← The Street, Aldermaston village. The home and practice of Dr Stanley Beale (1920-33) and subsequently of Dr Lionel Holmwood (1933-59).

Photo: Gazette Newspapers

↑ July 1983; Dr Joe Morland and his wife Nancy are presented with gifts to mark his retirement by Mrs Nora Goody of Tadley Parish Council. The people of Tadley turned out in force to thank him for the care and attention he had given his patients during his 32 years as General Practioner in the area.

← Dr Stanley Beale who practised from his home in Aldermaston between 1920 and 1933. He attended patients in the north Tadley area. On his retirement he sold the practice to Lionel Holmwood for £4,915/10s/0d.

War years

The British loss of life in the Great War of 1914-1918 was 750,000; the Tadley war memorial records thirty of these deaths. Tiny though this might seem compared to the national figure, it made a considerable emotional impact on a population of about 1400. In such a small community these men were familiar figures and their loss was keenly felt. In Tadley the peace celebrations following the end of the war shown on page 117 were genuine expressions of relief and hope for the future. While we may not be able to identify many of those who lived to celebrate the end of the Great War, we can recognise amongst others old Tadley families in the names of those who died: West, Saunders, Rampton.

The Great War was fought far away, or so it must have seemed at the time to a people who rarely left the area in which they were born. Except when tragic news came from the Front, life went on pretty much as normal in Tadley. Inhabitants could provide most of their own daily needs, so contact outside the local area was limited. World War II however was to prove very different. The war intruded on life in rural communities in various ways, changing it for ever. During the war Tadley people took part in the service and sacrifice demanded of the Home Front: joining the Home Guard, hosting evacuees, enduring rationing and shortages. Nearby Pamber Heath lost two of its inhabitants to German bombs. In the armed forces six Tadley men lost their lives.

In all of this Tadley was similar to other villages in the country. That is, until 1942, when the USAAF came to Aldermaston Airfield – the 'Yanks' had arrived! They would stay until 1945. Although some of the land that disappeared under runways, aircraft hangers, ammunition dumps and recreational blocks was in Aldermaston, it was on Tadley that the impact was greatest. There were dispersed military sites as far south as New Road, a pass was needed to get beyond the top of Mulfords Hill and the postmistress in that area sometimes had to have a military escort (who came in useful helping to deliver the mail!). The pubs, if they had beer, lured American soldiers with more money than the locals and Tadley girls also attracted attention from the GIs.

Little remains of these times of war in Tadley. Here and there can be seen the remains of wartime buildings, for example what became Tadley's cinema, The Royal, was airfield 'Building 205'. To walk down the concrete section of Blakes Lane is to be with the ghosts of GIs who regularly marched along the road nearly sixty years ago. The names of Winston Avenue and Franklin Avenue are tributes to wartime leaders. Tadley people still have vivid memories of those times of conflict – there are even a few old enough to recall World War I.

↑ One of the six Tadley men who lost their lives in World War II. Able Seaman Stanley 'Stan' Bowman had not long celebrated his 21st birthday when the launch he was in struck a mine.

Tadley has not had a strong military tradition and early photographs are rare.

↑ 'Will' Nash, 1905-08 Royal Field Artillary, during excercises on Salisbury Plain, riding *Esme* the 'best groomed' horse that day. The following day *Esme* was ridden on parade by King Edward VII.

← L/Cpl Luke Hawkins Appleton, of Shyshack Lane, served with the Gloucestershire Regiment in France and Italy during World War I. The Gloucester Regiment was raised in Portsmouth in 1694 as 28th of Foot. In 1802, after the Battle of Alexandria, it gained the unique distinction of wearing the 'back' badge on shakos (head dress) later cap. Also it is the only regiment to protect their colours by forming a square around them facing outwards – even the monarch, taking the inspection, has to march outside of the four sides.

Locally World War I had little impact – the nearest military activity was at Bramley Munitions Camp and Park Prewett Hospital, No 4 Canadian General Hospital. However, many locals served in the forces and Tadley's war memorial records the 30 who lost their lives.

↑ Soldiers from the 2nd Battalion Dragoon Guards (Queen's Bays) pictured in France during World War I. They are believed to be the only surviving members of the battalion. Pictured second from right, middle row, is local man (Leslie) David Englefield of Franklin Avenue.

← A photograph of 'boy soldiers', possibily taken in Basingstoke. There are several local lads in the photograph: back row (l to r): ?, Charles Stacey, ? Webb, ?, ?, ?, Raymond Stacey; middle row: Alf Stacey, ? Smith, ? Webb, ?, ? Saunders, Louis James; front row: ?.

↑ World War I ended on 11 November 1918, however the formal peace treaty (Treaty of Versailles) was not signed until 1919. These three photographs show scenes from the local celebrations when decorated horse-drawn floats, with folks in fancy dress formed part of a victory procession. The picture above shows a banner being carried with the caption 'TO THE BRAVE BOYS OF TADLEY'.

← Here are some of the walking contingent in the parade, with another float following. This 'Darby and Joan' couple are believed to be James Thatcher, local photographer, and his wife.

← In this view the lady with the bicycle is Mary Hicks and the two ladies in the centre, dressed identically, are Hilda and Ruth Rampton who ran one of the laundries in Heath End. It is thought that fireworks also formed part of the celebrations.

Prior to World War II the area now occupied by AWE was part of the Aldermaston Estate (see page 25). In 1941 the land was aquired by the government, cleared of woodland, and Aldermaston Airfield built.

↑ (top) Aldermaston Airfield being handed over by the RAF to the Americans in October 1942. Initially it was intended as a training base for RAF bomber crews. Soon after its completion, plans for an invasion of Europe were drawn up and the Americans arrived.

↑ (bottom) Primarily a transport base, various American units were stationed at Aldermaston during the war. This 1943 photograph shows a CG-4A glider being towed by a jeep of the 315th Airborne, who were stationed at the base between December 1942 and November 1943.

Life must have seemed strange for the many Americans based at Aldermaston during the war. Local historian, Gordon Timmins, has contacted many of them and recorded their wartime memories.

↑ (top) An informal photograph of four American servicemen taken outside one of the buildings on the airfield; (l to r): Bill Langstaff, Tom Towers, Ed Sullivan and Andrew Henderson.

↑ (bottom) The interior of an airfield accommodation building. Conditions seem basic – a single heater in the middle of the room – but were better than at many other bases!

Aldermaston Airfield was involved in several important missions during the war including D-Day and Operation Market Garden in 1944. On D-Day, planes and servicemen from Aldermaston were amongst the first to cross the Channel.

↑ Horsa gliders with their tugs lined up ready for D-Day. Note the rings on the aircraft fuselages which were unique to the D-Day missions – used as a means of identifying friendly aircraft. Prior to the start of the landings servicemen were living in a huge 'tent city' in the area now known as Newchurch Road.

← General McAuliffe, 101st Airborne (left), with Col W B Whitacre, September 1944.

↑ The wartime airfield impacted on local life in numerous ways. Many locals worked as civilians on the airfield. Between 1942-45 an American Red Cross canteen was run from the back room of building 223, subsequently the old Community Centre (see page 107). Left to right: Daisy Jewitt, Marjory Pike, Ida Willington (née Hutchins), Mrs Watson, ?, ?, Vera Cottrell, Sue Hammond, ?, Mrs Dawson and Phoebe Hicks.

← An informal photograph of two American servicemen on guard duty, outside an air-raid shelter. In the background can be seen airfield buildings.

The Vickers Collection, Rolls-Royce plc

↑ (top) Totally separate from the Aldermaston Airfield, in an enclosed compound, was the Vickers Supermarine dispersal site at Hangar 5 (now Hangar Road). Between 1943-46 Spitfire aircraft were assembled there from parts manufactured throughout southern England.

↑ (bottom) Not only did the airfield comprise the area now occupied by AWE, it extended south covering large parts of Tadley. Locals living inside the airfield boundary had to have a pass to enter or leave!

Many local people served their country during World War II. Those eligible saw active service, others carried out essential work at home.

↑ (left) George 'Curly' Saunders served as a Local Defence Volunteer (Home Guard). He is seen here carrying an actual rifle, replacing the earlier broomstick, which probably dates the photograph to 1942 or after.

↑ (right) A photograph taken in 1941 just before Geoff Dykes (age 20) left for Burma with 79 Fighter Squadron. On returning in 1946 he served with the underground operations room at Uxbridge.

← Home on leave just prior to D-Day, June 1944, are Roy and Arthur Nash pictured here with their mother. The field behind is now the Esso garage on Mulfords Hill.

During the 1920s many towns
and villages erected memorials
to honour those who had died in
World War I. Tadley's memorial
was originally located in what
is now a Memorial Garden near
Hicks Close.

↑ A view of the memorial in its
original location surrounded
by open land.

→ A wet, but well attended,
Armistice Day service from the
mid-1930s. In the background
are the converted railway
carriages which once stood
at Trunkpond Corner (Rowan
Road).

→ In 1963 the war memorial
was moved from its site near
New Road to land adjacent to
the Memorial Hall, The Green.
Watching the final stage of its
journey are (l to r): Henry
?, Peter Keep, Joyce ?, John
Stacey and his father George H
Stacey and Freddie Barrington.
George Stacey (junior) is
operating the chaseside. The
memorial stone was moved to
St Paul's Church in 1967.

↑ (top) Members of the newly formed local branch (1926) of the British Legion leaving their headquarters (The Fox & Hounds) for an Armistice Day remembrance service at the war memorial. The prefix 'Royal' was given by Her Majesty the Queen in 1977. The procession is led by either Col Johnson-Smith or Col Lynden-Bell with behind (l to r) Bert Layley, ? , and Frank Smith.

↑ (bottom) In 1949 a branch of the womens section, The British Legion, was formed in Tadley (re-formed 1984). This parade, women at the rear, is making its way from The Fighting Cocks to St Saviour's Church (see page 56) for the dedication of the women's standard. Leading members in the parade are: Alfred Rolfe (Snr), Freddie Br(e)akspear(e), Sandy Ogden, Ernest Nash, Ray Lock(e), Charles 'Nobby' Clark(e), Bert Layley.

Behind the wire

British Crown Copyright 2001/MOD

Over the years the Atomic Weapons Establishment (AWRE/ AWE) at Aldermaston has been know by many names, some more complimentary than others! The one we have chosen – 'behind the wire' – is well known amongst local people and highlights the mystery of the place. For many, the place that took over and dominated the life of Tadley from the 1950s onwards was mysterious – those who worked there were guarded about what they did and those who did not work there knew very little about what went on 'behind the wire'.

By our own definition for this book AWRE/AWE is not really in Tadley at all – most of the site lies in the adjoining parish of Aldermaston – but it has had such a dominating influence on Tadley since the early 1950s that it is impossible to ignore .

After World War II Aldermaston Airfield had a succession of occupiers, including an aircrew training centre operated by British Overseas Airways – a forerunner of British Airways. In the late 1940s Britain decided to develop its own nuclear weapon and a suitable site for the work was sought – the existing weapons research site at Fort Halstead being too small. Aldermaston was neither the original nor the preferred site but was finally chosen and 'handed over' on 1 April 1950.

The early 1950s were dominated by three tasks: constructing the site buildings, designing and building nuclear weapons, and developing the supporting infrastructure in and around Tadley. The wartime development of the airfield had a dramatic effect on Tadley but was nothing in comparison to the changes brought about by AWRE/AWE – within a very short period of time it was transformed from a small rural community into a modern town. Hundreds of new houses were constructed for AWRE staff, new schools were opened, existing shops expanded and new ones opened. Overnight the population of Tadley increased dramatically with the arrival of construction staff, scientists, engineers and support staff (eg police and fire). These staff either moved permanently into the new housing being built, lodged at the site hostel – Boundary Hall – or were 'bussed in' daily from the surrounding towns and villages.

When Aldermaston was established in the early 1950s it was one of several sites involved in nuclear weapons development (along with Foulness, Cardiff, Burghfield, Woolwich Common and Orfordness). Today, Aldermaston is one of only two sites in the country still working on nuclear weapons. The world is a very different place from those early days. The majority of the photographs included here have come from the AWRE/AWE archives; 50 years ago the level of support and co-operation this book has received would never have been allowed. Although the work carried out 'behind the wire' is probably as 'secret' as it always has been, AWE is far less 'secretive' about how it goes about its work and is more integrated into the life of the local community.

↑ Sir Winston Churchill visits the AWRE Aldermaston site in 1957. Churchill had been Prime Minister at the time of the Cabinet decision to develop a British hydrogen bomb in July 1954.

British Crown Copyright 2001/MOD

British Crown Copyright 2001/MOD

↑ An aerial view of the Aldermaston site taken in August 1953 by the RAF. The main runways can be clearly seen. Note Aldermaston village at the bottom left hand corner of the photograph and the embryonic Tadley housing estate at the mid-right.

← An aerial view of the Aldermaston site and the new Tadley housing taken by the RAF in August 1953. The airfield control tower can be seen in lordly isolation adjacent to the upper one of the three hangars in the centre-left of the photograph. Some of the wartime buildings are still standing near to Hangar 5 at the centre right. Heather House (see page 133), built specially for the AWRE Director, is situated in the centre foreground. At the far end of the Tadley housing estate, alongside the straight line of the A340 to Basingstoke, is a group of wartime buildings used as a hostel. Even in those days, this group was known as Boundary Hall.

British Crown Copyright 2001/MOD

British Crown Copyright 2001/MOD

↑ (top) One of the mobile kitchens used on the Aldermaston site during the first few years of its construction. This picture was taken in 1951.

↑ (bottom) An 'adequate' canteen was seen as an early priority and one was opened on the Aldermaston site in 1952. The interior has been refurbished and re-arranged on a number of occasions but the outside differs little from this view taken in May of that year.

British Crown Copyright 2001/MOD

British Crown Copyright 2001/MOD

↑ (top) The AWRE Main Library Reading Room in the period 1954-59, before the present semicircular extension was added. This area is still in use and is occupied by the extended bookshelves. The original tubular framework supporting the roof in this picture can still be seen.

↑ (bottom) The completed extension to the AWRE Main Library pictured in mid-1959. When the new extension was opened in 1960, it considerably increased the floor space and allowed most of the library services to be brought together under one roof.

British Crown Copyright 2001/MOD

↑ (top) An aerial view of the Boundary Hall complex taken just before it was demolished in August 1995. Originally based in the wartime Instructional Site No 1 buildings (see page 105), modern accommodation was built piecemeal, from about 1959 onwards, probably starting with the block nearest to Barclays Bank (see page 81). It gained its name because of its proximity to the Hampshire-Berkshire border.

↑ (bottom) A photograph from the early 1950s of a line-up of the buses operated by the Mountain Transport Services Company who were contracted to convey AWRE employees to and from the site.

British Crown Copyright 2001/MOD

Between 1951 and 1960 the Ministry of Defence built 2,300 houses spread over an area including Earley, Basingstoke, Calcot, Thatcham, Newbury and Tadley.

↑ (top) A July 1955 photograph of Priors Road on the Tadley housing estate. Most interesting are the white bands painted round the trunk of the tree on the right of the photograph: these were wartime blackout precautions.

↑ (bottom) Looking northwards along Heather Drive – part of the staff housing development. In the distance wartime buildings are still in evidence on the perimeter of the new AWRE site.

British Crown Copyright 2001/MOD

British Crown Copyright 2001/MOD

↑ (top) Sir William Penney, first Director of AWRE, pouring beers for servicemen present at the 1953 Totem Trial at Emu Field in Australia. The fine suit he is wearing was not his usual dress for Australian trials and indicates that he may have had an important meeting or engagement immediately before this more informal event.

↑ (bottom) An interior photograph of Penney's office, taken in about 1954. The inside of the main gate and a car park can be seen through the windows.

British Crown Copyright 2001/MOD

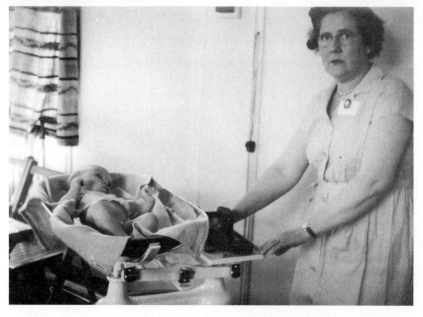

↑ (top) A view of the south-western elevation of Heather House, built in 1951 to accommodate the Director of AWRE; Dr and Mrs Penney lived there for eight years. It was sold to a private buyer in 1965 and subsequently demolished as a result of a fire in 1995. The site has since became a seeABILITY centre.

↑ (bottom) In the early years at Heather House, Eleanor, wife of William Penney, was actively involved in making life for the wives of AWRE employees more pleasant and stimulating. As an ex-nurse she exercised fully her skills on behalf of the young mothers – visiting and helping out at the baby clinic.

British Crown Copyright 2001/MOD

↑ The William Penney Lecture Theatre, built in 1964-65 as part of the AWRE Recreational Society complex. It is used for lectures, demonstrations, concerts and occasionally by various local organisations. *The Boundary Players* have continually used it since it was formally opened by William Penney in February 1966.

← Scene from *The Rape of the Belt* by Benn Levy, staged by *The Boundary Players* in 1961, using the costumes from the West End production. Seen here are Jean McKeown (left) and Pam Terry (right). During her 40 years with the group Pam acted in over 70 productions, playing a variety of roles, from 'dolly birds' to old ladies, always displaying great professionalism. In later years she also produced and directed over 30 plays for the company.

↑ A scene from *The Liberators* by Iain MacCormick, depicting the living room of a farmhouse in Northern Italy. Originally written for television, *The Boundary Players* were granted first option to stage it. The 1964 cast: (l to r) Maurice Dubras, Ted Welsh, Maureen Dillon, William White, Cliff Mason, Norman Smiles, Patricia Hogg and Keith Percival.

→ *The White Carnation* by R C Sherriff was performed in 1962. This photograph shows some of the cast with, on the right, Peter Todd. Peter was not only an accomplished actor and director but he designed and built most of the sets.

→ The backstage team responsible for transforming the bomb-damaged shell of a house to the scene above in the fastest major set change in *The Boundary Players* history. The regular wardrobe mistress, Angela Old is third from left and the long serving lighting and effects man, Allan Wilding, is seated on the floor third from right.

British Crown Copyright 2001/MOD

↑ (top) A 1959 dinner in the AWRE Staff Canteen in honour of Sir William Penney – Sir William can just be seen at the far left of the row of diners nearest the curtains. Amongst the others dining are Drs Challens and Levin (future AWRE Directors), Charles Adams (AWRE Chief Scientist), John Corner (Head of Theoretical Physics), Admiral Brooking (AWRE Assistant Director), Alec Frazer (theoretical physicist), Sir William Cook (former Deputy Director), Dr Ken Allen (nuclear physicist) and Stan Abercrombie.

← Another social occasion, taken in the same venue and year, showing some of the younger members of staff enjoying themselves at a New Year dance. All the ladies in the photograph and some of the men worked in the various drawing offices on site.

British Crown Copyright 2001/MOD

British Crown Copyright 2001/MOD

↑ A recent picture of Decoy Pond on the AWE Aldermaston site. Gordon Timmins, a local historian, has produced a history of this particular feature, which reveals that it is at least two hundred years old. It was used in a complicated process to trap a variety of wild fowl intended for the table. The process involved the use of tame ducks to entice the wildfowl into the trap, hence the name 'Decoy Pond'.

← The north-east corner of the Aldermaston site is home to a National Monument – Grim's Dyke – believed to be a part of the Roman defences of nearby Silchester. As a National Monument, it has to be preserved and protected from any damage.

British Crown Copyright 2001/MOD

British Crown Copyright 2001/MOD

↑ The Prime Minister, Harold Macmillan, paid a visit to the Aldermaston site in August 1957. He is shown here being introduced to Dr Bob Batchelor by Dr Ken Allan, Senior Superintendent, AWRE Nuclear Physics Branch.

← The first ingot of plutonium cast at AWRE Aldermaston in 1952. This was required for the core of the first British atomic bomb tested on 3 October 1952.

British Crown Copyright 2001/MOD

British Crown Copyright 2001/MOD

↑ The bare Aldermaston centre site in the early 1980s before the start of construction on a new complex of buildings that now dominate the skyline. This was the largest construction project ever carried out by the Establishment. Two of the original three main runways can be seen. The remains of the third can also be traced by following the long straight road that runs behind the large buildings in the foreground, adjacent to what was once a airplane taxiway.

← A89 under construction. Part of the AWE Centre Site facilities under construction in the mid-1980s.

← The almost completed AWE Centre Site buildings pictured in the late 1980s. These buildings include a new facility for handling and fabricating plutonium components.

British Crown Copyright 2001/MOD

Ted Baker

The year after Britain tested its first H-Bomb in the Pacific Ocean (1957), the Campaign for Nuclear Disarmament (CND) was formed and for many years AWRE Aldermaston and the annual Easter marches became the centre of attention for those supporting the abolition of nuclear weapons.

↑ (top) Easter 1958; the first Aldermaston March and the only one to march from London to Aldermaston. The photograph shows members of the 5,000 protesters as they reach their destination.

↑ (bottom) Easter 1963; protesters gather at Falcon Field before the start of the march to London.

Ted Baker

Ted Baker

↑ Easter 1963; marchers assemble around the forecourt of The Falcon public house (see page 33). By this time the march had become an annual event under the cry 'Ban the Bomb'.

← Easter 1963; addressing protestors is Canon John Collins who, with Bertrand Russell, launched CND. According to *Peace News*, 11,000 marchers gathered at Falcon Field, swelling to 17,000 on Saturday and 30,000 by Easter Monday. Approximately 70,000 attended the final rally in London. The last Aldermaston March was held in 1964, the year Canon Collins resigned as Chair of CND.

Page 5 *Tadley School, Standards II and III, c1930*

Back row standing (l to r): Mr Miller, Stan Baker, Eric Monger, Harry Monger, ?, Doug West, Jimmy Henstridge, ?, Bernard Stone, Doug Ward, Arthur Camp, Jimmy Hedger, Patience Williams, Miss Crief, Mabel Long, Peggy Trussler, Clara Pike, Clara Taylor; back row seated:, ?, ?, Ernie Keep, Jack Hobbs, Teddy Evans, William Rampton, Leslie Gundry, Donald West, Ellen Monger, Beulah Thatcher; middle row: ?, Mary Layley, Emily Saunders, ?, Esther Bowman, ?, Gilbert Cotterell, Freddie Chapman, Reggie Brocks, Vera Bowman, ?, Mary Chandler; front row: ?, Marjory Cottrell, Frances Lambden, Elsie Cook, Lily Hawkins, Harry Kite, ?, Lily Hawkins, Ada Cotterell, Gladys Cook.

Page 9 *Burnham Copse Infant School*

Top row (l to r): ?, Damon Clerk (?), ?, Lavinia Weston, James Anscombe, ?, Philip Watts, Katherine Smallwood, Russell Raisey (?), Gaila Adair (?), Ian Skinner (?); middle row: Imogen Grubb, Alison Mead (?), ?, Linda Christmas, Jill Hardy, Rona James (?), ?, ?, ?, Susan Martin, Caroline Rich (?); front row: Mark Pope, Mark Kennigan, ?, Julian Kent (?), ?, ?, Glyn Rolfe, Peter Burkwood (?), John Andrews (?), ?, John McKenna.

Page 38 *Outing to Southsea 1920*

1: Herbert Smith, 2: Lucy Smith, 3: Jessie Kimber (née Rose), 4: Ernest Kimber, 5: ?, 6: ?, 7: ?, 8: ?, 9: ?, 10: ?, 11: Elsie More, 12: Arthur More, 13: Ada Lambden, 14: Dorcas Hunt, 15: Vera Hunt (little girl), 16: Winnie Rye (née Kimber), 17: Alice Monger, 18: Mercie Kimber (married Fred Hunt), 19: Annie Smith, 20: ? Annie Thatcher, 21: ?, 22: Doris Kimber, 23: ?, 24: Baby Joy Smith, 25: ?, 26: John Gault, 27: Keith Gault, 28: Lizzie Gault, 29: Rose Kimber (nanny), 30: Elsie Kimber, 31: Edith Kimber, 32: Lizzie Kimber, 33: Fred Cotrill (?), 34: ?, 35: Grace Smith, 36: Ern Smith, 37: Samual (Bert) Rose, 38: Will Thatcher.

Page 38 *Old Meeting outing to Southsea*

1: ?, 2: Jim Monger, 3: Gilbert James (Boys' Sunday School Superintendant), 4: Annie James (Gilbert's wife), 5: Eli West, 6: Elizabeth West (Eli's wife), 7: ?, 8: ?, 9: ?, 10: Elizabeth West (Albert West's mother), 11: Leah Stacey, 12: ?, 13: ?, 14: ?.

Page 39 *Outing to Southsea 1927*

1: Mrs Bowman, 2: Mrs Bowman, 3: ?,
4: Jock Hudson (driver for Kents, recruited
from the workhouse), 5: Marjorie Nash,
6: Mrs Nash (mother of Marjorie), 7: Brenda
Nash (Marjorie's sister), 8: Alice Stroud,
9: Mrs Ford (organiser of the trip), 10: ?,
11: Nancy Stroud, 12: Minnie Saunders,
13: Mabel Fell (née West), 14: ?, 15: ?, 16: Alice
West, 17: Dolly West (daughter of Alice),
18: Mrs Stroud, 19: Iris West, 20: Mabel
Saunders, 21: Tony Edwards, 22: ? Barlow.

Page 47 *Tadley Band*

1: ?, 2: ?, 3: ?, 4: ?, 5: ?, 6: Jack West, 7: Gideon
West, 8: Will Thatcher, 9: Mr Nicholson,
10: ?, 11: Albert Lambden, 12: Ernie Bowman,
13: Barnet Saunders, 14: Ernie West.

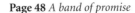

Page 48 *A band of promise*

In uniform Top row (l to r): John Kimber,
Ernie Kimber, George Tull, Alec James, Herbert
Monger, John Lambden; middle row: Arthur
Monger, Fred Hunt, Bert Saunders, Charlie
Lambden, Fred Monger, Gilbert James, Tom
Cottrell; front row: Will Lambden, Frank
Lambden, Tom Lambden, David Norris, Barnet
Saunders, Henry West.

Non-uniform Charles Lambden (left), Arthur
Kimber (right).

Page 50 *Tadley Band 1937*

Top row (l to r): Brian West, Dennis
Monger, Bernard Stone, Ted Hutchins, Norman
Lambden, Gideon West, Reg Bowman, Arthur
Carpenter, Ernie West; middle row: Ernie
Smith, Stanley Bowman, Arthur Smith, Ernie
Kimber, Ernie Bowman, Fred Hitchins, Donald
West, Leslie Saunders, Tom Chapman, Roy
Dent; front row: George Carter, Percy Savery,
Will 'Dickie' West, Joseph Dyson (professional
coach), John Lambden, Charlie Lambden,
Frank Lambden, Charlie Rivers.

Acknowledgements

A book of this kind could not have been produced without the support of numerous people; the Project Team (Peggy Anscombe, Bob Brown, Ian Burn, Alan Cooke, Pat Galvin, Malcolm Isted, Carol Stevens, and Derek Ward) owe a considerable debt to all those who have given so generously of their time and knowledge. Without their contribution the book would have been the poorer. We hope it does credit to the wealth of fascinating photographs and information they so freely supplied. It will be obvious to many of them that we have only been able to include a fraction of the photographs they contributed – we hope they agree with our selection.

Special thanks go to the members of Tadley and District History Society who helped and supported the project from its inception.

Permission to reproduce photographs from their collections has kindly been given by AWE Aldermaston, The Francis Frith Collection, Gazette Newspapers, National Monuments Record, Newbury Weekly News (Peter Bloodworth), Reading Chronicle, Reading Evening Post, Reading Museum, Rolls Royce plc, Rural History Centre, Southampton Museum of Aviation, Trinity Mirror plc.

We would like to record our warm thanks to those who loaned personal photographs and provided information: Peggy and Jim Anscombe, Les Appleton, Stan Baker, Elsie Beavers, Bishopswood Infant School, Bishopswood Junior School, George Blake, Rosey Bond, Maurice Bound, Roy and Daphne Bowman, Wendy Brant, Ann and Mike Broad, Dr Peter Brough, Bob Brown, Ian Burn, Burnham Copse Infant School, Burnham Copse Junior School, Burnham Copse WI, Jean Butler, Jean Chapman, Pam and Dudley Cook, Hazel Dore, Geoff Dykes, Guy Elliott, Ted Englefield, Emlyn Evans, Kath Eyles, Cath Farrow, Lou Fell, Mabel Fell, Kath Gethin, Brian Gooch, Gwen Goode, Jean Gundry, Joan Hancock, Ruth Hoar, Hurst Community School, Paul Lacey, Joyce Lambden, Bill Langstaff, Avril Massey, Nancy Morland, Bob Morrison, Arthur Nash, Roy Nash, Mrs Nicholson, Val Norris, Carol Nottage, Harold Pippin, Wendy Rawlings, David Rose, Beryl Sandford, Gordon Saunders, Brian Scutter, Joan Searing, St Mary's Church, David Stacey, Iris Stanley, Carol & Jim Stevens, Joan Stevens, Tadley Band, Tadley Community Primary School, Tadley Town Council, Mike Targett, Pam Terry, Andrew Thompson, Gordon Timmins, Alf Rolfe, Derek Ward, Pat Ward, Major Sylvia Watchorn, Albert West, Ethel West, Margaret Lane, Pam West, Stewart Whatmore, Frank Wickens, Jimmy Williams, Ida Willington, Angie Wilson, Fred Woltman. To preserve their privacy, ownership of individual photographs loaned to us will not be disclosed to third parties.

We have made every effort to contact the owners of photographs used in the book. If we have been unsuccessful, we invite the copyright holders to contact us.

We would like to record the ready assistance from the staff at the following libraries and archival repositories: Basingstoke Library, Cambridge University Library (John Wells), Hampshire Record Office (Janet Rooms), Rural History Centre (Caroline Benson and John Gilmore), Tadley Library, Willis Museum (Ernie Major).

Many other people have assisted in the production of this book, but the following deserve a special mention: Alf Rolfe who did so much of the leg-work, researching information and photographs; several Departments at AWE and the Ministry of Defence for the supply of images for the 'Behind the wire' chapter; Kate Pyne for her support and enthusiasm for the project from the outset; David Bearne for the unlimited use of his photographs; Jean Burn and her trusty iMac for her secretarial support and help with the typing; Jo Stevens for her input into the design of the cover.

Many people helped with the checking and proofing of the book. Ann Broad, Alison Burn, Keith and Pauline Buckingham and Vickie Ward all spent time checking for errors – spelling, grammatical and factual. Any mistakes that still remain after all their efforts are the responsibility of the Project Team!

The book was designed and typeset by Tadley and District History Society members; their task would have been far greater without the professional help and advice of Fred Amner – in particular when choosing the type of paper to use!

Finally, our grateful thanks to Hampshire County Council and Awards for All for their financial assistance towards the cost of printing the book.